THE GREAT CRUSADE

THE GREAT CRUSADE

A Guide to World War I
American Expeditionary Forces
Battlefields & Sites

Stephen T. Powers
Kevin Dennehy

GTCI Press
Denver, Colorado

Published by GTCI Press

ISBN-13: 978-0997110517

Kevin Dennehy dedicates his efforts to his old unit, the 29th Infantry Division, one-third of whose members became casualties in only 21 days of combat during World War I.

Steve Powers wishes to dedicate his efforts to these mentors:

The U.S. Naval Academy

Paolo E. Coletta
James Arnold

The Rice Institute

Hardin Craig, Jr.
Frank E. Vandiver
Floyd S. Lear

The University of Notre Dame

Marshall Smelser
Leon Bernard

ACKNOWLEDGEMENTS

We would like to extend our heartfelt thanks to the following individuals who contributed to *The Great Crusade*'s research, production and successful Kickstarter campaign.

William Andersen
Russ Battiato
Ron Berger
Lawrence Berrick
Jim BrownTomas
Laurie Button
Christopher Davis
Barbara DeCoster
Regina DeCoster
Jude De Lorca
Ronald Diz
Clem Driscoll
Alan Enslen
Susan Fishbein
Mary Fitz
Norm Frickey
Paul Gannon
Robert Gilliland, Jr.
Larry Goodman
Stephen Habib
Mark Lachniet
Sherman Leibow
Charlie Loan

Robert Massa
Jack McKenna
Ellen McMullen
Judith Miller
Leroy Montoya
Maureen Reilly
Michael Rauen
Tomas N. Santos
Patricia Shapiro
Felix Schütz
Michael Sheldrick
Christopher Sluss
Frank Steiger
Dave Taylor
Trish Tolentino
George Thrower
Debra Veilleux
Jeff Weingard
Robert Woodard
Eric Young

TABLE OF CONTENTS

MAPS

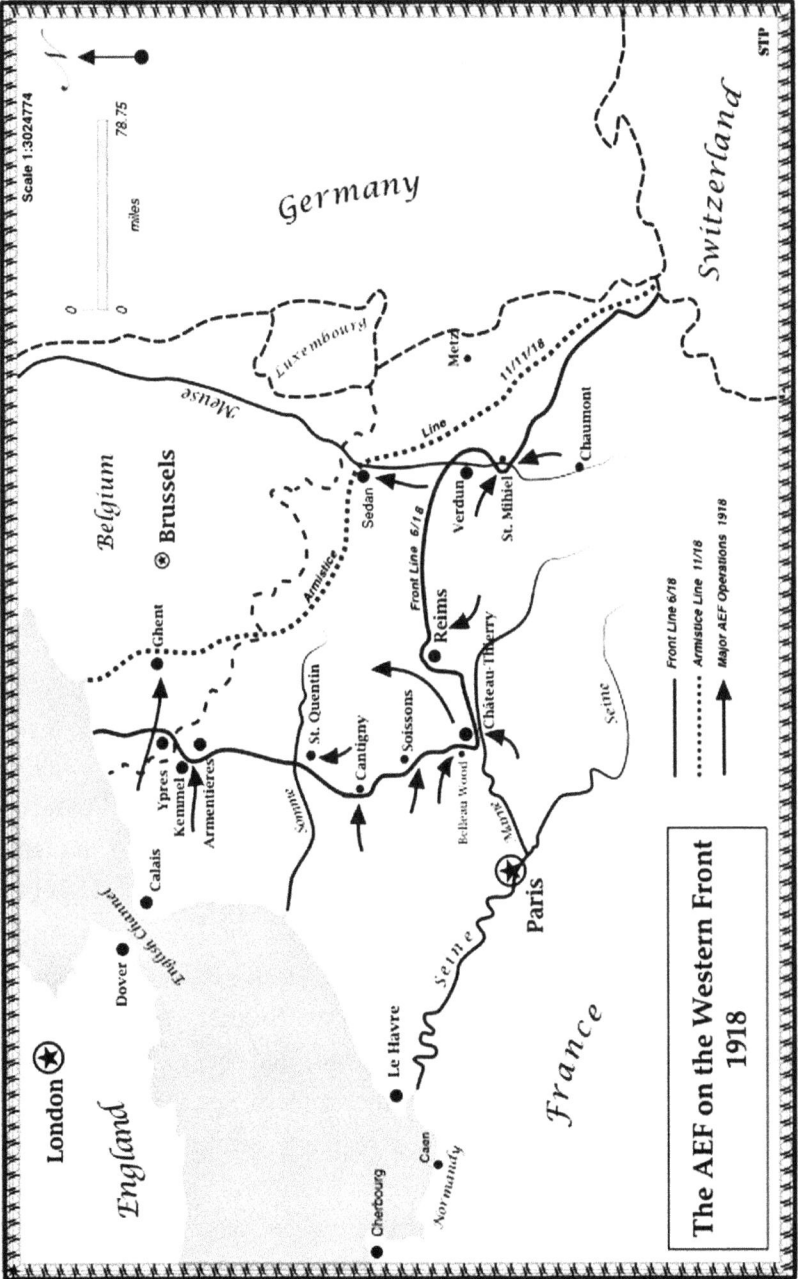

The AEF on the Western Front
1918

INTRODUCTION

Over there, over there,
Send the word, send the word over there -
That the Yanks are coming,
The Yanks are coming
The drums rum-tumming everywhere
So prepare, say a prayer
Send the word, send the word to beware -
We'll be over, we're coming over,
And we won't come back till it's over
Over there.
George M. Cohan   1917

On an overcast day in November 1921, the 11th day to be exact, a large number of American dignitaries, generals, newspaper reporters and interested citizens gathered along with President Warren G. Harding in Arlington National Cemetery to dedicate the Tomb of the Unknowns, a memorial to the almost 117, 000 American soldiers, sailors and airmen who had died in combat during World War I, the Great War, 1917-1919.   Especially honored as pallbearers for the Unknown Soldier were a handful of carefully selected doughboys who had been awarded the Congressional Medal of Honor, among them Sgt. Alvin C. York, Lt. Samuel Woodfill and three officers of the 77th Infantry Division (ID), Capt. Nelson M. Holderman, Capt. George G. McMurtry and Maj. Charles W. Whittlesey, who had earned that highest honor commanding "The Lost Battalion" in the Argonne Forest three years before.   With the possible exception of Alvin York, whose lasting fame was ensured by the 1940 Academy

Award-winning film, "Sergeant York," today these soldiers are virtually forgotten. Yet, their sacrifices, with those of their comrades-in-arms, were enormous: in a little more than five months of intermittent combat the American Expeditionary Forces suffered almost 321, 000 casualties of which 53, 513 were killed in action and another 71, 345 gassed. At one point in time there were 193,564 doughboys hospitalized from wounds, poison gas and diseases of all sorts.

So, the intent of this guidebook is to aid you in remembering these heroes, to guide you to the battlefields where they and hundreds of thousands of other doughboys fought, to help you locate the numerous scattered post-war memorials to their efforts and to visit the military cemeteries where so many rest today. We hope this guide will bring these forgotten soldiers and their exploits back into focus during this centennial year of America's entry into the Great War.

WWII battlefields, cemeteries and sites have dominated American military tourist destinations in Europe since the 1950s, leaving similar Great War sites increasingly forgotten, neglected and even vandalized. If it were not for the American Battle Monuments Commission, they would probably all would have suffered a similar fate. A million tourists visit the Normandy American Military cemetery overlooking Omaha Beach annually, while only a few hundred bother to visit the WWI cemetery at Suresnes on the outskirts of Paris or travel east 70 or so miles to the Aisne-Marne American Cemetery where so many U. S. marines who died in the Belleau Wood rest. Part of the reason, of course, lies with the passage of time. The number of Americans who were alive in 1917-18 and still with us is miniscule. Frank W. Buckles, the last American soldier who served during the Great War, died in 2011. The passage of time has certainly dimmed our memory of and interest in the battlefields of the Great War, if not those of our Civil War. Possibly, it's the proximity of the Gettysburg, Antietam,

Vicksburg battlefields, among others, which keeps that interest alive or, maybe it's just the nostalgia for a lost cause. Yet, if there were ever a lost cause, Woodrow Wilson's hopes that The Great War would be a "war to end all wars" that would "make the world safe for democracy" rank high on the list, yet evoke little nostalgia among today's cynical Americans.

A vandalized 1st Infantry Division Monument in the Argonne Forest.

Whatever the causes of our forgetfulness, we hope that this modest guide to the WWI American battlefields and memorials in Europe and the United States will spark a new interest in travel to these sites, off the main tourist routes as they may be. Many of these memorials are breathtaking; all are worth visiting for the memories, patriotism and sense of sacrifice they still evoke today.

While the emphasis of our guidebook is on American WWI battles, battlefield memorials and cemeteries in Europe (mostly in France), we have included other sections that we believe will be interesting to our readers, such as a list of museums and memorials in the United States and Canada's War Museum. Readers should note that most museums on active U.S. military posts that are home to WWI units will have a display devoted to the Great War, only a few of which we have singled out.

The literature on WWI is so vast that we have included a brief bibliography of accessible works for readers who would like to pursue further the military aspects of the war. In a different vein, we have also added a section listing feature films with the Great War as their background.

We would like to thank the many friends and acquaintances who have aided us in this project. Their help and encouragement have been invaluable, but any errors are our own.

Stephen T. Powers
Kevin Dennehy

Denver, Colorado
April 2017
www.militaryhistorytraveler.com

USING THIS GUIDE

"The Great Crusade" is not just a travel guide to the various American WWI battlefields in France and Belgium, it also contains chapters on America's entry into the war, the creation of the AEF and its battle history. We believe that we have done a bit better along the travel guide line than, for instance, "Fodor's France," which references WWI and Château-Thierry in a single sentence. Fodor's and other standard guides won't deepen your understanding of the Second Battle of the Marne or the U.S Marines' epic advance into the Belleau Wood. This guide will enhance that understanding and help make the Great War come alive in your imagination.

No guidebook remains current for long after its publication. Roads change, memorials are moved or vandalized and often new ones are dedicated. The authors will greatly appreciate hearing from you, the users of this guide, about its deficiencies, errors and omissions. Please use our website to share your thoughts and comments: www.militaryhistorytraveler.com.

Airfare to Europe
Depending on when you travel, airfare can be very expensive. Prepare for a round-trip Coach flight costing $1,000 or more (depending on what city you fly from). However, traveling during winter months and the shoulder seasons, April and October, will be cheaper. Surf a number of airline websites directly to compare prices as well as Kayak.com, Orbitz, Hipmunk, Airfarewatchdog and others, which will e-mail you updates when a price goes up or down. Discount carriers like WOW Air (wowair.us) offer rates to Paris as low as $149, each

way, from several U.S. cities. Low-cost carriers such as EasyJet and Ryanair fly many intra-city routes in Europe.

Car Rental and Driving

Because many of the battlefields, cemeteries and monuments are in rural Belgium and France, be prepared to rent a car for greater flexibility. Besides searching the usual sites such as Kayak, go to the European-based car companies' websites (Europcar, www.europcar.com). Public transportation such as trains and buses, while efficient in Europe, can be expensive and will rarely get you close to the sites in this book.

When driving in Europe, remember your speed. You won't be driving down the 1970s and 1980s German autobahns anymore, with their unlimited speed limits. Traffic cameras are frequent, and when they catch you speeding, the fines are expensive. You may not even get the ticket until months after the violation.

Tip: Take your valuables out of your rental car. Seems like common sense, but thieves prey on tourists all throughout Europe, especially at remote tourist sites.

Watch for signs in city centers; there are strict no driving, no parking zones. Tickets again are expensive. For both speeding and parking tickets, the car rental agencies are in cahoots with the local government and will automatically charge your on-file credit card.

Filling up at gas stations is expensive

Make a mental note when you leave an airport rental car agency as to the location of the nearest gas (petrol) station so you can top off your tank when you return; the monetary penalty for returning a car with an empty tank, as in the United States, is severe.

Tip: You can drive for miles in rural France without seeing a gas station. Do not leave a major highway without topping off your tank. Author Kevin Dennehy almost ran out of gas in the Argonne Forest because he could not find a gas station in any village near the Meuse-Argonne Cemetery. The cemetery's superintendent suggested a gas station 15 kilometers away. When Dennehy arrived, no one could speak English to tell him how to run the gas pumps. Luckily, a young French woman spoke a little English showed him how to gas up and pay with his credit card. Don't let your tank run dry—it will ruin a trip.

Google Earth

One of the newest, simplest and least expensive ways to find your way to the American monuments and cemeteries scattered around both Europe and North America is to use the various navigational aids provided by Google Earth Pro. The free app is easily downloaded onto any computer or mobile device and is relatively simple to use.

Getting driving directions from Google Earth goes something like this: Open the app. A box will appear on the left of your screen; the globe is on the right. At the top of the box, click "Get Directions" to view a dropdown tab with A & B lines. Type in your starting city (or village) on the A line and your destination on the B line, then click on "Get Directions" in the blue box. Up comes a scroll with a suggested route that includes road numbers, mileages and approximate driving time. Google often suggests secondary routes as well. Even more magical is that when you do this, the globe on the right will rotate and zoom in on the route, providing the same directions overlaying a blue line marking the route. If your plans are sufficiently well-developed before you leave home, all this can be done at your dining room table. The information provided in the earth view is vast and programmable, including museums, places of interest, war memorials, etc. Use it to the fullest.

It's really that simple. Give it a try before you leave on your trip by typing in "Château-Thierry, France" on the A line and "Croix Rouge Farm Memorial, France" on the B line. Google will come up with the somewhat complicated driving directions in a few seconds. In the case of names that are repeated in a country or appear as the same in several countries, be sure to include the name of the country or province (state) as we have done in this example.

For the truly GPS-literate we have provided coordinates for many of the individual sites.

You may still want to have a conventional map by your side as a backup. There are many choices, but you won't go wrong with one or more of the Michelin Regional maps (the larger maps of France don't have sufficient detail). On Amazon they sell for $11 to $13 new with used copies available.

Passports and Credit Cards
Ensure your passport is up-to-date. That seems like basic information, but how many times have you looked at the expiration date? Even to book most international flights, you will need to have a current passport number. Credit cards are necessary in Europe. Visa and MasterCard are the most accepted, so tell your credit card company that you are going overseas (also find out if the card has an international surcharge that can add up). Bring an ATM card because that is the easiest way to get Euros (and it offers a better exchange rate than airport currency vendors). Make sure your ATM card is chipped; many European terminals will only accept that variety and they are safer.

Cell phones
Find out if your carrier has a European calling and data plan. This beats calling from a hotel with high land-line rates. Also, it is good for Google Maps to help you navigate both small villages and big cities. If you don't have access to Google Maps, splurge to rent a GPS navigation unit for your car.

Lodging
Besides Kayak, TripAdvisor and Orbitz, don't forget to use such sites as Airbnb for week or longer rentals. They can be much cheaper than hotels and you will be able to better experience the culture of the village or town you are staying in as you will be interacting more closely.

Food
It's France. You can find bad food, but that's your fault. Consult TripAdvisor, but also use other sources such as Rick Steves, Frommer's, Fodor's and other guides.

Packing
In the heavily forested Argonne, the weather can go from sunny to torrential rain very quickly. Pack cold-weather gloves, coats and hats in the winter months. Have wet-weather gear (ponchos, umbrellas, etc.) in other seasons. Wear comfortable walking shoes/boots. Pack a small first-aid kit. Despite all the above, pack as lightly as you can. From the moment you arrive at your departure airport, you will begin to love that lighter bag.

Tying in history with a vacation
Not everyone shares our enthusiasm for military history, so couples and families may be overwhelmed with the many battles, monuments, cemeteries and other war memorials. By combining a trip to the Champagne region, using Reims as a base of operations (see our tour recommendations), there are many non-military sites, cathedrals, Roman ruins, museums, and vineyards. For example, Château Thierry is on the southern edge of the Champagne region, with its many *vignerons* producing the sparkling wine. (Only sparkling wines from this region can be legally labeled "champagne" in the EU.) The area between Château Thierry, Epernay and Reims make up the famous Route Touristique du Champagne (the Champagne Route).

Roman gate in Reims.

East of Reims, the Argonne, besides the site of the famous 1918 AEF battle, is a fascinating area to explore.

The U.S. war memorials, while remote, are also near Luxembourg, Holland, Germany and other European Union nations with their many non-military tourist and historic attractions.

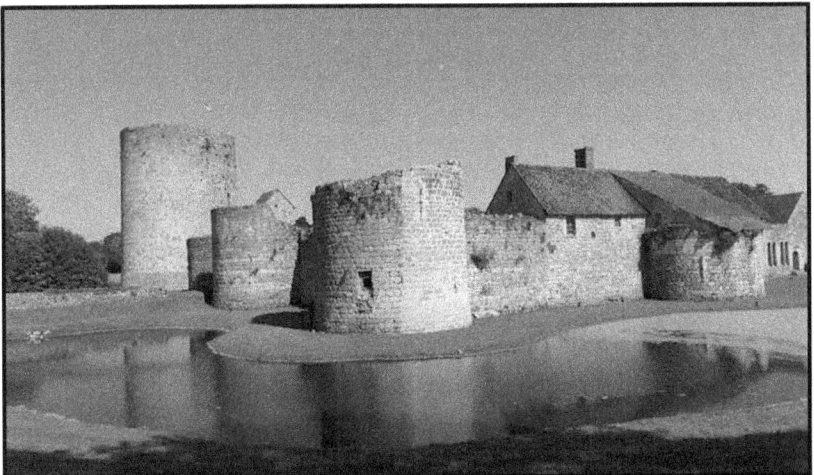

Medieval castle near Oise-Aisne Cemetery.

AMERICA GOES TO WAR, 1915-1917

At 2:10 in the calm, clear afternoon of May 7, 1915, *Kapitänleutnant* Walther Schwieger, commanding the German *Unterseeboot U-20*, submerged a few kilometers off the south Irish coast, caught sight of a large passenger liner that had seemingly appeared out of nowhere steering east toward the St. George's Channel leading to Liverpool.   Schwieger set a converging course and eventually closed the distance to torpedo range. He then ordered a single torpedo fired. *U-20*'s laconic log entry records the appalling result: "Clear bow shot from 700 meters. ... Torpedo hits starboard side close abaft of the bridge, followed by a very unusually large explosion with a violent emission of smoke. ... The ship stops at once and very quickly takes on a heavy list to starboard, at the same time starting to sink by the bow. She looks as if she will quickly capsize. ... The ship blows off steam; forward the name Lusitania in gold letters is visible. Funnels painted black, no flag on the poop. Her speed was 20 knots."

RMS Lusitania, a flagship of the Cunard Line, sank within 18 minutes of being torpedoed, ending the lives of 1195 passengers and crew, including 94 children and 140 Americans. Despite a warning from the German Embassy, published in New York newspapers before she sailed, that *Lusitania* was carrying munitions and Canadian soldiers, thus forfeiting her "passenger ship" status and making her subject to attack as a belligerent warship, public opinion outside the Central Powers, and especially in the United States, condemned the attack as a gross violation of the rules of war. World opinion in 1915, already shocked by alleged German atrocities as its army overran neutral Belgium, was as yet unaccustomed to the ruthlessness of the maritime war now being waged by German U-boats.

German depiction of Lusitania torpedo attack (Photo: Wikimedia)

The reaction of American President Woodrow Wilson was immediate. Since his proclamation of American neutrality the previous fall, he had striven to maintain that stance, hoping to keep the United States "neutral in fact as well as in name, impartial in thought as well as action," but now he sent notes to the German Foreign Office demanding that the *Kaiserliche Marine* (Imperial German Navy) cease its U-boat attacks on ships carrying passengers and non-contraband goods. His demand was largely ignored as the *Admiralstab* (German Imperial Admiralty Staff) persisted in its U-boat campaign for another four months, further alienating world, and especially American, public opinion already being manipulated by British propaganda.

Wilson's decision also prompted the resignation of his Secretary of State, William Jennings Bryan, who counseled a more even-handed policy toward the belligerents. Bryan's successor, Robert Lansing, a State Department lawyer specializing in international law, was staunchly pro-Allies.

The U-boat campaign had come in response to Great Britain's undeclared blockade of northwestern Europe. As the world's dominant sea power, the British had earlier refused to sign the Declaration of London in 1909 (concerning the rules of naval warfare) because it feared that to do so would limit its ability to wage an effective blockade of a continental enemy. When the United States proposed in 1914 that the warring powers now sign the Declaration, the British Foreign Office again balked and, with the help of its friends in Washington, had the proposal quietly quashed. The blockade being waged by the Royal Navy now included virtually anything an enemy could use to wage war, going far beyond the old ban of weapons and munitions, even if those prohibited goods were being shipped to a neutral nation. The State Department sent numerous notes to the Foreign Office protesting the violation of our perceived rights as a neutral to trade in non-contraband of war with any nation, anywhere, belligerent or not. The British executed their blockade very cleverly so as not to bring about a rupture of diplomatic relations with the United States, e.g., they let cotton through to the Continent so as not to anger southern Democrats in Congress and paid fair market prices for the cargoes they confiscated. Even so, most Americans felt that the nation's sovereignty and its status as a world economic power were grossly compromised.

The Germans responded by declaring the waters around the British Isles a war zone in which they would attack all shipping with no regard to flag. Since British ships used the ruse of flying neutral flags to disguise their identity and were often armed as well, the Germans could make a case for their policy. U-boats were also limited by their vulnerable construction, and by their small number. The *Kaiserliche Marine* could only deploy a dozen or so of its 50 available U-boats at any one time. The German naval buildup that had been ongoing since 1900 had concentrated on capital ships (battleships and battlecruisers), rather than U-boats; with hindsight, that decision was a major strategic mistake.

In 1915, the U-boat war shifted to the Mediterranean where they took an alarming toll on Allied shipping. Since few ships flying the Stars and Stripes plied Mediterranean waters, a diplomatic crisis with Germany was averted temporarily. However, in February 1916, a desperate Germany declared that all armed ships (the British Admiralty had been arming merchant vessels for some time), either neutral or belligerent, would be subject to attack by U-boats, and then shortly thereafter bungled its threat by torpedoing the unarmed French cross-channel ferry, *Sussex*, injuring several American passengers. The Wilson administration responded by sending the German Foreign Office a note demanding that German submarines either cease attacking non-military ships or the United States would be forced to sever diplomatic relations. The Imperial General Staff once again backed down, acceding to all of Wilson's demands in a note that became known as the Sussex Pledge. By this action, the *Admiralstab* reluctantly agreed to end its submarine campaign. But, the Pledge itself was a snare for the United States for, if violated, Wilson's threat of breaking off diplomatic relations would inevitably lead to war, a consequence that the president still wished to avoid.

Behind all the administration's diplomatic maneuvering (Wilson sent his close personal advisor, the pro-Allied "Colonel" Edward House to Europe several times to ascertain if there were any terms on which the warring powers could agree to end the conflict), a preparedness campaign, fueled in large part by the Republican Party, was gaining strength. That campaign bore fruit in two important pieces of legislation, the National Defense and Naval Appropriation Acts of 1916. Both pieces of legislation displayed a shocking misreading of America's true military and naval needs in response to two years of European war, but they at least started the country down the path to preparedness. It must be said, however, that most Americans in 1916, including their representatives in Congress, neither wanted nor expected war. We will deal with these two pieces of legislation and their shortcomings in a later section of this work.

President Woodrow Wilson (Photo: Wikimedia)

In June of 1916, Wilson was re-nominated by the Democratic Party at its St. Louis convention. The keynote address was delivered by former New York governor, Martin Glynn whom Wilson had asked to stress preparedness and Americanism. As Glynn began a recital of the Administration's efforts to keep the country out of the European war, the delegates shouted "What did we do?" leading Glynn to shout back "We didn't go to war." Thus was born the winning Democratic campaign slogan "He Kept Us Out of War." In November, Wilson defeated the Republican candidate, the somewhat stolid, conservative, former New York governor and Supreme Court justice, Charles Evans Hughes, by the razor-thin margin of 600,000 votes (277 to 254 votes in the Electoral College).

By the time of his re-election, Wilson may have kept the United States out of the war, but the country was far from neutral. The British blockade of the Central Powers enforced by the Royal Navy's control of the high seas had meant that trade across the Atlantic flowed readily to the Entente Powers, but was choked off to Germany and its allies. While the administration formally protested the British blockade as a violation of America's neutral rights, by the end of 1916, American corporations and banks, through the sales of food and munitions financed with loans, were tied to the military fortunes of Great Britain, France and Russia. Still, the United States might have stayed out of the conflict if, in early 1917, the German High Command had not gambled on starving Britain into submission by launching a new "unrestricted" submarine campaign against all shipping, neutral as well as belligerent entering a self-designated "war zone" around the British Isles. t lost its gamble.

In January 1917, when the German offensive the previous year at Verdun had not brought about the collapse of the French Army, an Imperial Council meeting at the Kaiser's castle in Pless made the fateful decision to resume unrestricted submarine warfare on February 1 with the object of finally starving Great

Britain to her knees. As for the possible reaction of the United States, neither Army nor Navy commanders were concerned. Admiral Henning von Holtzendorff, chief of the *Admiralstab*, argued that the U-boats would not only cripple the British economy in five months, but would also prevent an American army from reaching France. Further, even if Americans did cross the Atlantic in significant numbers, the Imperial General Staff discounted both the fighting ability of the individual American soldier and the laughably undersized and ill-equipped U.S. Army. The war would be won, both German staffs believed, before the Americans could influence its outcome. Of course, both staffs were terribly wrong.

Gen. John J. "Black Jack" Pershing (USMA, 1886) (Photo: Wikimedia)

Carefully timed to forestall American protests, German Ambassador Johann-Heinrich von Bernstorff presented Secretary of State Lansing with a note detailing his government's decision on January 31. The German public announcement of the resumption of unrestricted submarine warfare came the next day. Faced with this affront to Wilson's idealistic hopes for a just peace, laid out in a January 17 address to the Senate, his dream of brokering a peace – "a peace without victory" – now dead, Wilson severed diplomatic relations with Germany in early February. Although the peace faction in Congress blocked his proposal to arm American merchant ships, Wilson used his executive power after Congress went into recess to order that arming anyway, inaugurating a short-lived policy of armed neutrality.

In short order, U-boats sank three American ships with the loss of American life, whereupon, backed unanimously by his Cabinet, the beleaguered president called Congress into special session.

At this critical moment, German Foreign Secretary, Arthur Zimmermann, committed a breath-taking blunder by sending a note to his ambassador in Mexico instructing him to inform the Carranza government of the resumption of unrestricted U-boat warfare and offering to help financially in the re-conquest of the American Southwest if Mexico would join the Central Powers in attacking the United States in the event of war. Furthermore, Zimmermann also suggested that Japan might be invited to join in the attack. Given the mobilization of the National Guards along the border and Gen. John J. "Black Jack" Pershing's excursion into northern Mexico in pursuit of Pancho Villa, the proposal might not have seemed as far-fetched in 1917 as it does today.

British naval intelligence (Room 40) had been able to decode parts of the message that had been sent to Count Johann von Bernstorff, the German Ambassador to the United States, on

January 16, but its director, Capt. William R. "Blinker" Hall, RN, kept the contents secret until the moment was ripe. That moment came on February 19 when the note was shown to diplomats in the American Embassy in London. Wilson's subsequent release of the "Zimmermann telegram" on February 28 through The Associated Press news service (to hide its British source) shocked and angered the nation, overwhelming the existing anti-war sentiment, especially since Zimmermann held a press conference the next day during which he admitted sending it. (With a certain Teutonic arrogance, Zimmermann informed the *Reichstag* a few weeks later that Germany would finance Mexico's war only in the event that the United States declared war on Germany.)

Now that the Tsarist regime in Russia had been swept away by revolution, the path was open for the United States to join the two Entente democracies in their fight against German authoritarianism and barbarism.

At 8:30 in the evening of April 2, 1917, Woodrow Wilson and his second wife, Edith, escorted by a troop of cavalry, were chauffeured down Pennsylvania Avenue to deliver his war message to Congress. There was a light rain falling as he entered the Capitol and mounted the podium to address the joint session. Wilson called on Congress to declare war not just for the violation of America's neutral rights on the high seas, but for a higher moral purpose, saying that the United States would fight "for the things we have always carried nearest to our hearts – for democracy, for the right of those who submit to authority to have a voice in their own government, for the rights and liberties of small nations" ... "It is a fearful thing," he concluded, "to lead this great peaceful people into war, into the most terrible and disastrous of all wars, civilization itself seems to be in the balance."

The anti-war faction held up congressional action for four days, delaying passage of the declaration of war until April 6, when the United States entered the war as an Associate Power of the Allies. In the critical vote, six senators and 50 members of the House voted against the resolution, including Republican representative Jeannette Rankin of Montana, the first woman elected to a seat in Congress, a pacifist and suffragist who broke House rules by announcing as she cast her vote that "I want to stand by my country, but I cannot vote for war."

Of course, the Wilson administration could have avoided war by knuckling under to German demands and prohibiting American citizens and ships sailing under the American flag from entering the war zone. The Scandinavian nations stayed out despite U-boat attacks on their commerce and citizens by doing something similar. Woodrow Wilson, by taking the moral high ground, took his unprepared nation to war not just to preserve the profits of American corporations and banks, but as he memorably said, to make the world "safe for democracy."

Thus, the American people went to war as they had so often in the past (and would again in the future), divided and militarily unprepared. It has been their habitual way of making war.

Sites connected to "America Goes to War":
When we last checked the U.S. Capitol Building, where President Wilson delivered his war message and where the Congress actually voted that a state of war existed with the Imperial German Empire, has not yet been put on the auction block or leased to help pay off the National Debt. Tours of the Capitol Building are available with strict security restrictions. See the website listed below.

For the next two years, the U.S. Capitol Visitor Center is offering an exhibit titled "Congress and the World Wars" that displays political cartoons, posters and constituent correspondence "to see how Congress responded to the issues facing the nation …" during the war years.

The Center is located beneath the East Front Plaza and is open

Monday through Saturday, 8:30 a.m. to 4:30 p.m. Closed Thanksgiving, Christmas, New Year's and Inauguration Days. For more information go to www.visitthecapitol.gov.

RMS Lusitania lies on her starboard side under 300″ of murky water 11 miles off the Kinsale Lighthouse, Ireland, where she came to rest. The badly deteriorated vessel seems in danger of collapsing on itself, probably from secondary explosions in her longitudinal coal bunkers.

One of her salvaged screws is on display in the foyer of the Hilton Anatole in Dallas, Tex., USA. Another is on display at the Merseyside Maritime Museum in Liverpool, England. A third is still attached to its shaft and the fourth was melted down as salvage.

There is a memorial in the town square of Cobh (the former Queenstown) to the victims of the *Lusitania* disaster. There is now a second, newer memorial and garden on Old Head of Kinsale, now a spectacular private golf course. The memorial is located off the west side of R604 as it leads down to the Lighthouse near the ruins of the Old Head signal tower. Many of the 1916 victims are buried in Cobh's St. Multose Church cemetery. A memorial stone to Margaret Mackenzie was dedicated there as recently as 2016.

The conning tower and deck gun, salvaged from the wreck of *U-20*, are on display in the Strandingsmuseum St. George in Thorsminde, a town on Denmark's West Jutland coast. *Kapitänleutnant* Schwieger ran her aground in early November 1916; unable to get her afloat, he blew off her bow with his torpedoes. *U-20* remained visible for years, attracting tourists in large numbers. Today, the wreck lies about 400 yards off shore and is no longer visible.

The State of New Mexico maintains the Pancho Villa State Park on the site of old Camp Furlong outside Columbus. Several of the old buildings from 1916 are preserved on site, including the old Customs House that now houses the Visitor Center.

Exhibits include displays dealing with the life and career of Pancho Villa, the 1916 raid itself and the U.S. Army's Punitive Expedition. The Village of Columbus and Camp Furlong are on the National Register of Historic Places and come under the jurisdiction of the National Park Service.

Columbus is located on the New Mexico/ Mexico border, 35 miles south of Deming off New Mexico Rt. 11.

The Park is open year round from 8:00 a.m. to 5:00 p.m. Small admission charged.

For further information: Phone: (575) 531-2711, Websites: nps.gov or columbusnewmexico.org.

CREATING THE AMERICAN EXPEDITIONARY FORCES

It was one thing for the Wilson administration to take the nation into war against the Central Powers in April 1917; it was quite another to project American military power across the Atlantic in time to influence the war's outcome.

However, some progress toward military preparedness had been made since the guns of August boomed in 1914. Because of congressional action in 1901, the Regular army had been increased to 106,000 officers and men by 1915, more than five times the number under arms at the outbreak of the Spanish-American War in 1898, but only a tenth of the force needed to constitute a modern, effective army in 1917 terms.

Since 1915, former Army Chief-of-Staff Leonard Wood and Republican ex-president Theodore Roosevelt had been waging a preparedness campaign calling for increases in both military and naval appropriations through organizations such as the Army League, the Navy League, the American Rights Committee and the National Association for Universal Military Training. Much of the argument over preparedness seems arcane to us today with considerable ink and verbiage being spent over the nature and control of the state militias and whether they could be sent overseas to fight a foreign war. When the dust settled, Congress had agreed on a compromise measure known as the National Defense Act of 1916. President Wilson duly signed it into law on June 3, 1916, which, coincidently, was the day he learned of the indecisive clash of British and German dreadnoughts off the Jutland peninsula.

The NDA of 1916, for all of its compromises, was the most comprehensive piece of military legislation in the nation's history. It rejected the idea supported by many advocates of the preparedness campaign by defeating the proposal, advanced by Secretary of War, Lindley M. Garrison, for the creation of an Army reserve organization to be known as the Continental Army, a force totally under the control of the Federal Government and the U.S. Army. Instead, Congress favored a bill, known as the Hay Plan, which would keep the state National Guards as the Army's principal reserve, but would clarify their legal status by giving the U.S. Army control over their training, equipage, officer's commissions and especially would permit their use outside the continental United States when called to federal service.

Wilson's supported Hay's bill, really having little choice, which prompted the resignation of both Garrison and his Assistant Secretary. The president then quickly asked Newton D. Baker, the former progressive mayor of Cleveland who had no background in military matters, to take over the War Department. It turned out to be a fortuitous choice for the diminutive, easy-going Baker worked well with both congressional Democrats and the Army brass. On March 23, the bill passed in the House by a majority of 402 to 2. In addition to the provisions regarding the National Guard and other reserve units, the NDA also authorized the increase of the Regular Army to 175,000 officers and men over five years, a ridiculously small number for the war it would soon be asked to fight.

Passage of the Hay bill by the House hardly ended the controversy over national security as the next day a U-boat torpedoed the channel ferry *Sussex*, reigniting the Senate debate over the creation of the Continental Army. The Senate quickly produced a bill endorsing that plan. Both bills went to a House-

Senate conference committee where the differences were resolved in favor of the House version.

Shortly thereafter, the Senate passed a House naval appropriations bill authorizing the construction of eight new capital ships, the largest naval expansion in American history, to create "a navy second to none". The U.S. Navy was already the third largest in the world in number of modern battleships and battlecruisers, none of which were going to be of much use in its upcoming war against the U-boat. Left out of the Naval Act of 1916 were the various types of anti-submarine craft that were needed to win this upcoming battle in the Atlantic.

All this congressional infighting played out, not just the struggle in Europe, but also against American meddling in the ongoing revolution in Mexico. Ostensibly to protest the brief arrest of a shore party of American sailors at the Gulf port of Tampico in April 1914, the U.S. Navy landed a force of sailors and marines at Veracruz. Embarrassed by the incident, the Wilson administration turned to international arbitration to work out an agreement allowing it to extricate the Army troops who had replaced the marines. Further meddling led one of the revolution's charismatic leaders, Pancho Villa, to raid Columbus, New Mexico on March 9, 1916, killing 10 civilians and eight soldiers from the 13th Cavalry Regiment. The War Department responded by sending Gen. Pershing with 5,000 regulars into Mexico in an effort to track down Villa. With the NDA now signed into law by Wilson, and anticipating further trouble (that came in the form of numerous additional raids across the Texas border by *Villistas*), the War Department federalized the state National Guards (first those of Texas, Arizona and New Mexico, and then a month later all the rest), sending them to patrol the southwest border. Viewed against the backdrop of the murderous battles raging in France on the Somme and at Verdun, neither effort reflected well on the state of American military preparedness. Unable to bring Villa to bay and after fighting an inconclusive battle at Parral against Mexican *Carrancistas*, Secretary Baker withdrew Pershing's force in February 1917. Mexican affairs were now allowed to cool, averting a war because tension with the German Empire had reached the breaking point.

Since the United States' stated reason for declaring war on Germany was the defense of its neutral rights, it was conceivable that the Wilson Administration might have fought a limited naval war, but national pride compounded by anger at the loss of innocent American lives dictated otherwise. No one in the administration, neither the president nor Secretary of War Baker, nor anyone in the military, really questioned the need to raise, equip and ship an enormous army to France to intervene decisively on behalf of the Allies. (The United States never formally joined the Triple Entente of Great Britain, France and Russia, but merely allied itself as an Associate power.)

Despite that resolution and all its efforts in 1916, the U.S. Army found itself woefully unprepared to fight a European war in 1917. On April 6, the Regular Army could only muster about 128,000 men and officers. The National Guard, with an authorized strength of 450,000 under the NDA of 1916, stood at 174,008 officers and men. Neither of these forces were at anything close to full strength, nor were they equipped to fight on the Western Front, almost completely lacking in aircraft, tanks and, most important, modern artillery.

Shortly after the declaration of war, a British delegation headed by Foreign Secretary Arthur J. Balfour arrived in Washington to press his country's case for immediate military aid. Soon thereafter, French General Joseph Joffre arrived with a French delegation to beg that some show of America's military commitment to the Allies be made immediately. In response, the War Department ordered four Regular Army infantry regiments, then stationed on the Texas and Arizona borders, to entrain for the east coast, where their ranks were filled with recruits and transfers from other regiments. Rebranded as the U.S. 1st Expeditionary Division (later the U.S. 1st Infantry Division), these four regiments, the 16th, 18th, 26th and 28th with three attached artillery regiments (minus most of their guns), began shipping out from Hoboken, N.J. in June for the 12-day passage to Saint-Nazaire. Gen. John J. Pershing, newly named to command the AEF, soon followed with a small staff in tow. A battalion of the 16th Infantry marched down the Champs Élysées on the Fourth of July still wearing their wide-brimmed felt hats, *les hommes au chapeau de cow-boy* to the cheering French crowds who lined the Avenue. After a month camped near Saint-Nazaire, the division moved to a French training camp near Gondrecourt, east of Paris, to learn the rudiments of warfare on the Western Front and close enough to the front to hear the sound of distant gunfire. There, they came under the tutelage of the French 47th Division of *Chasseurs Alpins*, the tough and experienced "Blue Devils," so named because of the color of their uniforms and their reputation in battle.

Meanwhile, Congress quickly moved to remedy the Army's manpower deficiencies by passing the Selective Service Act of 1917. Adjutant General Enoch Crowder designed the new system carefully avoiding the mistakes of Civil War conscription practices. Rather than provost marshals going door-to-door writing down the names of potential draftees, now all male citizens (or those planning to become citizens) from age 21 to 30 inclusive were called on to register at local selective service boards that were to be set up throughout the nation. Under Crowder's system there were no bounties, purchased exemptions or substitutions. Voluntary registration was required as an obligation of citizenship. On the last day of August 1917, the age limits of those subject to conscription were expanded to include all male citizens or citizens-to-be from 18 to 35. Volunteers in the draft bracket from 21 to 30 were accepted into the Army until December 15; the following August all voluntary enlistments in the Army ended, followed shortly by enlistments in the Navy and Marine Corps. By November 11, 1918, the draft had accounted for 67 percent of the manpower in the armed forces, with almost one out of five drafted Americans being foreign-born. The draft had also spurred voluntary enlistments while that route remained open.

Resistance to the draft was minimal, but very real nonetheless. Just under 4,000 draftees attempted to establish their status as conscientious objectors; of those, 2,599 accepted alternate, noncombatant service of some sort. Eventually, 504 conscientious objectors who would not serve in any capacity were court-martialed by the Army. Death sentences were meted out to 17; another 441 received sentences ranging from life to ten years imprisonment with lesser sentences being handed out to the remainder. It was all bluff: no conscientious objectors were ever executed and by November 1920 all had been released from prison.

The Army quickly created 33 cantonments, spread across the nation from Camp Shelby near Hattiesburg, Miss., to Camp Devens outside Ayer, Mass., to receive and train the new inductees. Other camps were used for training officers, marines and aviation specialists. Usually, each division was assigned to its own cantonment, but others, such as Ft. Meade, Md., were used to train follow-up units. In Meade's case, both the 79th and the 93rd Divisions trained there. The Meade cantonment area, marked by a bronze signpost, is now the Fort's golf course.

The size of these cantonments, given the time span in which they were thrown up, is astonishing. Camp Funston, located on the grounds of Ft. Riley just outside Manhattan, Kan., where the 89th Division and other units trained, consisted of 1,400 temporary wooden buildings and tents that sat on 2,000 acres and there, some 50,000 men underwent basic training. The first Army cases of the Spanish flu were reported at Camp Funston in March 1918.

The army that was thus created, partially trained and then deployed to Europe, the American Expeditionary Forces (hereafter AEF), originally consisted of three distinct parts: the Regular Army (RA), the National Guard (NG) and the draftee National Army (NA). Note: Some present-day authors refer to this American army as the American Expeditionary Force, however we have chosen to use the contemporary term.

Gas masks had to be produced in mass quantity. (Photo: Wikimedia)

Regular Army divisions were numbered 1 through 8. National Guard divisions carried numbers 26 through 42, but their regiments lost their Civil War designations and were now numbered in the 100s. The draftee National Army divisions carried numbers from 76 to 93 with their regiments' assigned numbers in the 300s. In August 1918, the ruthlessly efficient Chief-of-Staff, Maj. Gen. Peyton March, issued an order that largely erased the distinctions among the three forces in matters of command, administration and insignia. There had already been so much intermixing of personnel that, combined with the flood of replacements, the original designations were no longer viable. Thereafter, the name "U.S. Army" applied to all.

All those infantry divisions consisted of two brigades of two regiments each with an additional brigade of artillery (two regiments, one equipped with 105 mm and the other with 75 mm cannons). Additional battalions of engineers, machine-gunners, signal and various rear echelon units brought this "square" division to about 40,000 men. Allied generals thought them cumbersome, but "Black Jack" Pershing had designed them as fighting units that could remain effective in combat despite taking heavy casualties, something that smaller British and French divisions had failed to do.

By November 1918, the 3,685,458 man AEF was organized into two armies (1st and 2nd) with seven corps containing 41 divisions. It was a remarkable mobilization from the Army's prewar strength of 213,557 men in all the Regular Army and National Guard units.

Raising manpower for the AEF turned out to be much easier than training, equipping and shipping it to France. Without considerable help from the British and the French (and, we might add, the U.S. Navy) the half-trained AEF would have languished state-side waiting to be issued weapons and provided transport while the decisive 1918 battles were being fought on the Western Front.

Gen. Pershing firmly believed that a lengthy training program was necessary to turn callow, young American men into adequate, if not quite professional, soldiers. The problem Pershing faced was that there wasn't enough time to train over three million recruits up to his standards.

(Note: Nor were the "open warfare" tactics that Pershing and staff at GHQ strongly advocated, based on infantrymen advancing in lines or by flanking maneuvers carrying bolt-action, magazine rifles tipped with bayonets, with incidental support from artillery, tanks or aircraft, very relevant to 1918 fighting on the Western Front where limited-objective-infiltration attacks with machine guns, gas, automatic rifles, mortars, grenades and covered by artillery barrages now dominated. Yet, Pershing complained several times in his memoirs of the lack of doughboy rifle training. Undoubtedly that training, limited as it was, paid off in thousands of firefights, as exemplified by those of Alvin York and Sam Woodfill, but field officers soon learned that courageous American doughboys armed with rifles and bayonets were no match for Boche machine gun nests laying down barrages from dozens of Maxims. The casualties from those "open warfare" tactics could not be sustained.

This lack of realistic training would cost tens of thousands of doughboys their lives against a more experienced Boche foe. The Yanks who poured through French ports by the hundreds of thousands in 1918 had anywhere from four months to a few weeks training, not the six months to a year thought necessary in the pre-war Army. Not even Regular Army and National Guard units could be said to have been adequately trained since many of their men, officers as well as enlisted, had been commissioned or recruited after April 1917. The problem extended up the chain of command as Pershing found many field-grade officers unequal to his expectations and relieved them promptly.

M1903 Springfield rifle (Photo: Wikimedia)

Those General Officers relieved of their commands in France included three division and four brigade commanders as well as a corps commander. (Officers relieved from duty reported to the

Classification Depot in Blois for reassignment, often a ticket home to a training billet, and were said to have been "Blueyed".)

Military equipment of almost every description was nonexistent or in short supply, nor, as it turned out, could those deficiencies be easily remedied.

Take the matter of infantry weapons. The standard American shoulder arm was the 1903 Springfield rifle, arguably the best bolt-action, magazine rifle possessed by any contemporary army. The rifle played a key role in the Army's proposed battlefield tactics. Army planners envisioned "open" as opposed to trench warfare, a fluid battlefield in which infantry formations would maneuver against the enemy relying on accurate fire from their riflemen for striking power. Hence, U.S. Army infantry training, unlike that of European armies, stressed rifle marksmanship as a key element.

The problem in 1917 was that the Springfield Armory and the Rock Island Arsenal had produced only 600,000 Springfields. Production facilities could not be expanded quickly enough to meet the new demand. Fortunately, a number of American private arms manufacturers had been producing hundreds of thousands of Lee-Enfield rifles for the British Army, so as British demand tapered off in 1917, it was relatively easy for them to retool to produce Lee-Enfields chambered for the American .30-06 round rather than the British .303. Thus, the majority infantrymen in the AEF went into battle carrying Lee-Enfields (designated officially as the U.S. Rifle, caliber .30, Model 1917).

The story is much the same for the three excellent automatic weapons John Browning designed for the U.S. Army: the Model 1911 .45 cal. pistol; the Browning Automatic Rifle (BAR); and the .30 cal. water-cooled machine gun. When war came, there were only 68,533 Model 1911 .45 pistols in the Army's inventory and, while contracts were signed with a number of prominent arms manufacturers including Remington, Winchester and

Springfield Armory, none was able to deliver the required pistols. One assumes that the deficit was made up with the many different revolvers in service use before the adoption of the Model 1911. In the close quarters fighting in the trenches during 1917-18, the handgun may have come of age as an infantry weapon. They were routinely carried on patrols into no-man's-land and on trench raids.

While handguns might be useful in close combat, light automatic weapons were essential for trench warfare tactics, but few BARs ever reached the front line troops before October 1917; instead, doughboys were forced to rely on greatly inferior British Lewis and French Chauchat automatic rifles.

Browning's excellent water-cooled, .30-06 caliber machine gun, the M1917, likewise reached the AEF too late to affect the outcome of the 1918 battles. American machine gun battalions were armed with the French air-cooled Hotchkiss, chambered for the 8mm Lebel cartridge. It weighed a hundred pounds and required an eight-man crew to service, but at least it was reliable and could fire 450 rounds a minute.

Artillery presented a similar problem. Contracts were let to American firms for the manufacture of artillery pieces (but, surprisingly not the Midvale Steel Company, already producing gun tubes and carriages for the British) that none managed fill before the Armistice. American artillerymen went into the Meuse-Argonne battle in the fall of 1918 firing French-made 75mm cannon and their longer-range 105mm and 155mm howitzers, and not enough of the latter.

Tank and aircraft production was mostly a failure. The Ford Motor Company was under contract to produce 15,000 light tanks; when the war ended, it had manufactured 15. A cooperative project between the British and American manufacturers to produce 1,500 30-ton tanks was scheduled for 1919.

Capt. Eddie Rickenbacker (Photo: Wikimedia)

American aircraft production was also a joke, sometimes a deadly joke. The AEF's Air Service received 1,213 De Havilland 4s made in the United States; unfortunately, the aircraft's nickname was "the flying coffin" because of the propensity of its gas tank to explode on landing. American pilots, often with a minimum of training, flew French and British aircraft. (America's top ace, Capt. Eddie Rickenbacker, first flew a French Nieuport 28 and then a SPAD S.XIII to rack up his 26 kills.) The Air Service established a pilot training complex at Issoudun, 157 miles south of Paris, which was at its height the largest such facility in the world. (Today nothing remains of the base except for a forgotten marker west of the city.)

The story is the same with merchant shipping. The American merchant fleet was small by world standards in early 1917 when the German unrestricted U-boat campaign began to wreak havoc on Allied shipping; losses came to over 2 million tons in February, March and April, two or three times the rate of replacement. Only when prodded by American Rear Adm. William S. Sims (USNA, 1880), whom the Secretary of the Navy, Josephus Daniels, detailed to London in early 1917 to liaison with the Admiralty, did the British reluctantly begin organizing convoys. Before 1917, the Admiralty thought an efficient, worldwide convoy system could not be organized.

With substantial government subsidies, American shipbuilding geared up to produce the bottoms needed to win the war, but its effort came too late. Even the 300,000 tons of shipping launched on July 4, 1918 had little impact on the war effort. American International Shipbuilding created the largest single shipbuilding yard in the world at Hog Island on the Delaware River near Philadelphia, but launched its first bottom on August 5, 1918, too late to be of much help in the war effort. Efforts to build both wooden and composite hull ships produced meager results as well, with only 71 coming off the ways. Over half the AEF was transported to France and supplied there by British troop and supply ships. The U.S. Navy seized German ships in American ports to transport most of the rest. Many thousands of doughboys were also crammed into U.S. Navy warships never intended for use as troop transports for the Atlantic passage.

Yet, the number of doughboys carried across the Atlantic was impressive. In each of the months from May through September 1918, more than a quarter of a million arrived safely in France. (Of the 1,100,000 American soldiers who crossed the Atlantic in British bottoms, only 637 were lost at sea. Two hundred and eighty-four additional doughboys were lost when U-boats sank American troop transports *Tuscania*, *Moldavia*, and the animal transport *Ticonderoga*, none sailing under the protection of the Navy's Cruiser and Transport Force.)

Gen. John J. Pershing arrives in France on June 13. From left to right: Gen. John J. Pershing, Gen. J. B. Dumas, Capt. James Lawton Collins, Brig. Gen. Etienne Pelletier and Gen. Pierre G. Duport. (Photo: National Library of Scotland)

Pershing eventually organized them into two armies of 14 divisions containing about 550,000 men (fighting alongside another 110,000 French *poilus*). No matter that their artillery, tanks and aircraft were of French manufacture and most of their rifles of British design, the Yanks had arrived.

Many of the difficulties the United States faced in training, equipping and transporting the AEF to France were alleviated by the appointment of two men to key positions in the war effort. Three general officers had held the position of Army Chief of Staff during the first year of the war. Only when Secretary of War Baker appointed Maj. Gen. Peyton C. March to the job did he find a man capable of bringing some order into the chaos the rapid expansion of the Army had caused. (Transportation problems became so serious at the end of 1917 that the U.S. Railroad Administration nationalized the nation's railroads for the duration of the war.) Baker found March, who was then serving in France with the AEF, just in the nick of time for the Congressional hounds were baying at his heels, publically calling for his resignation. March, a 53-year-old West Pointer (1888), was almost a perfect choice for the demanding job with his experience as a field commander in the Spanish-American War and the Philippine Insurrection and his time on the General Staff. To bring efficiency to Army administration, which he quickly did, March soon expanded the General Staff from its ridiculously low pre-war number of 20 to a thousand by November 1918 and combined its two divisions into one under the dynamic Maj. Gen. George W. Goethals, the officer who built the Panama Canal. March also made it very clear that he was the Army's senior commander and that everyone, including Pershing, answered to him.

The AEF continued its phenomenal growth through 1918 so that by November 1 it numbered more than 3,600,000 men. Its size would have increased beyond four million if the war had continued into 1919. Although often put off by March's abrasive nature, after the war Secretary Baker credited him with creating the military underpinnings needed to ensure victory.

The other individual who stepped forward to bring order into the morass of military/civilian procurement was the Wall Street financier and speculator, Bernard M. Baruch. Baruch's appointment to head the War Industries Board (on which he was already serving) came after the Wilson Administration had tried several other insufficient expedients. Sen. George E. Chamberlain of Oregon, chairman of the Military Affairs Committee, disgusted with the failings of the war effort, introduced a bill to create a War Cabinet in December 1917. That congressional threat to the administration galvanized Wilson and Baker into making their two key appointments of March and Baruch on the same day, March 4, 1918. In later passing the Overman Act in May, Congress virtually gave the president dictatorial powers over the reorganization of the economy, which Baruch put to good use. However, the war ended before the reforms March and Baruch put in place could be fully realized.

After his arrival in France in the spring of 1917, Pershing fought long and hard to keep his doughboys from being parceled out to reinforce weak spots in the Allied line. He strongly believed that the AEF could have the greatest impact on the military stalemate if it went into action as a cohesive entity under his command. No amount of cajoling or pleading by Gens. Foch, Pétain and Haig could change his mind or weaken his resolve. Only the military crisis precipitated by the German 1918-spring-offensive convinced him to release some of his divisions to French and British control. Pershing really had no choice; the Allied military situation was that dire. The insertion of American troops, green as they may have been, into the faltering Allied positions at Cantigny and especially at Château-Thierry and the Belleau Wood was instrumental in stemming the German advance on Paris. When that crisis had passed, Pershing again took control of most American divisions on the Western Front in preparation for the battles that would define the AEF's contribution to the defeat of Germany – the reduction of the Aisne-Marne and St. Mihiel salients and Meuse-Argonne offensive. Historian Russell Weigley wrote in his "The American Way of War" (1973) that the creation and preservation of the AEF was "Black Jack" Pershing's greatest military contribution to winning the war.

Black Soldiers in the AEF

The pre-war Army maintained several all-black units that had served with distinction in the post-Civil War period, most notably the "Buffalo Soldiers" of the 9th and 10th cavalry regiments. (The two post-Civil War African-American infantry regiments, the 24th and 25th, are today included under the "Buffalo Soldier" rubric.)

Soldiers of the 369th Infantry wearing French Croix de Guerre medals (Photo: Wikimedia)

Surprisingly, none of the black units in the Regular Army joined the AEF in France. The 9th Cavalry served in the Philippines, while the 10th spent its war years on the Arizona/Mexico border where it skirmished with Mexican irregulars. The 25th Infantry pulled the choicest assignment of all – garrison duty in the Hawaiian Islands.

The fate of the 24th Infantry was tragic. Sent to Houston, Tex. in the summer of 1917 to guard construction projects at Camp Logan, the regiment's enlisted personnel came into armed conflict with locals, including law enforcement officers. On August 23, in protest of what they believed had been the murder of one of their own, about 150 doughboys armed themselves against orders and marched on the town. In the fracas that resulted four soldiers and 15 civilians died, resulting in the convening of three court-martial boards that handed down death sentences to 14 soldiers and life sentences to 41 more. Jim Crow racism had reared its ugly head and determined the fate of thousands of young black men drafted into the U.S. Army.

Overall, the Army's effort to train black draftees in southern camps was a mixed bag. In deference to southern politicians, it tried to keep the ratio of whites to blacks in the camps at two to one. Jim Crow segregation was enforced everywhere. The situation became so tense at Camp Wadsworth in South Carolina that the commander of New York's 15th Regiment asked that his men be moved to a less hostile environment. Still, the all-black 8th Illinois Regiment, sent to Camp Logan under tight control after the riot, managed to survive without incident over the winter of 1917-18 before being deployed to France.

The African-American doughboys sent to France in 1917-18 were products of the Selective Service system. Out of this enormous black manpower pool (almost 368,000 inductees), the Army authorized the creation of only four regiments, (the 369th, 370th, 371st and 372nd) and one division (the 92nd), all of which experienced combat in France with varying degrees of success. Most black soldiers ended up in rear-area labor battalions working on the docks or in depots moving the tons of supplies needed to keep the AEF functioning. Often they were not given any real military training, but were just maintained, often poorly with regard to food and housing, as conscripted laborers.

Matters stood very differently with the four independent regiments; all served with the French where they experienced extensive combat. In fact, the 369th Infantry (New York's Harlem Hellfighters) was in action for 191 days, probably more than any other regiment in the AEF. The other three regiments, the 369th, 371st and 372nd, received high praise and Croix de Guerre unit citations from the grateful French under whom they served,

However, the history of the 92nd Division in France is tragic. Shipped to France in June and July, the Division spent the next two months occupying a quiet sector of the front in the Vosges Mountains. Pershing tapped it for a reserve role with the I Corps in the Meuse-Argonne offensive with the 368th Infantry assigned a liaison role with French Fourth Army on the far left of the American line. Initially that regiment, advancing on a battalion front, made good progress, but German resistance stiffened and the attack soon faltered with the lead battalion having returned to its start line by nightfall. Attacks ordered on September 27 and 28 fared little better, ending with the relief of the Second Battalion commander. Some advance was made on the 29th when the First Battalion was driven forward by its caucasian soldier-of-fortune commander, Maj. John N. Merrill, but the effort was too little and too late to prevent the relief of the entire division. After its failed attack, even the French wanted nothing to do with the disgraced division, which was sent into Army reserve, a permanent limbo.

The immediate aftermath became draconian when the Third Battalion commander preferred charges of cowardice against five of his officers. The Court-Martial Board found all five guilty, sentencing four to death and the fifth to life imprisonment. (The Board's sentences were later reversed and all five officers pardoned.)

A 1919 board convened to investigate the debacle and found many extenuating factors to explain the 368th's failures: poor maps, absence of artillery support, lack of wire cutters, difficult terrain and mission creep. The factors not mentioned were the abysmal training the division had received as a second-class Army unit and, more important, debilitating effects of the pervasive racism permeating American society and its Army at the beginning of the 20th century. Low expectations generated by racism inevitably produced the 368th's failures in the Argonne Forest.

The tragic history of the 92nd ID did not end with the debacle of 1918. The division was resurrected as the 92nd Infantry Division (Colored) in 1942 and eventually deployed to Italy in October 1944. There, it failed in an attack at the Serchio River and was again pulled from the line, reorganized (the 442nd Infantry [Nisei] was assigned to the division) and two regiments broken up.

The 368th Infantry had been stripped from the 92nd ID in 1942 and assigned to the 93rd ID (Colored). The 93rd was deployed to Guadalcanal in early 1944 where its regiments were parceled out among a number of backwater islands utilizing the African-American GIs as stevedores and guards.

Jim Crow was still alive and doing well in our "Greatest Generation."

CANTIGNY: THE AEF's FIRST BATTLE, MAY 28-30, 1918

As 1917 ended, Gen. Erich Ludendorff, now directing the entire German war effort from his official position as Quartermaster General, realized that his U-boat gamble had been a strategic failure. Not only had unrestricted submarine warfare not starved Great Britain into submission, it had failed to prevent the American Expeditionary Forces from reaching France. But now, the collapse of Tsarist Russia into revolution and chaos gave him one last opportunity for a decisive stroke to defeat the Allies on the Western Front. With numerous divisions fighting in Russia and Poland available for transfer to the west, he had the resources for a series of offensives that would pound the Allies into submission. He believed those *Soldaten,* employing new infantry and artillery tactics, would prove decisive. Ludendorff chose a British sector of the front on which to focus his first effort using the dubious logic that if the British could be knocked out of the war, the weaker French armies to the south would collapse as well.

Since it would be late spring before the Flanders sector would dry out enough for offensive operations against the British, he moved three armies, the 2nd, 17th and 18th, to the Somme front between Arras and the Oise River for the opening attack of his *Kaiserschlacht* (Kaiser's Battle). Those armies launched their offensive (codenamed "Michael") at 04:40 on a foggy Thursday morning, March 21, with intense artillery barrages from some 6,000 guns, before infiltrating specially trained *Stosstruppen* battalions, aided by the fog and gas, through the shattered positions held by the British 5th Army. The German advance continued for a week before WWI battlefield entropy and stiffening resistance brought it to a halt at the crossroads town of Montdidier about 40 km south of Amiens. To strengthen the flank of their salient, the Germans also occupied the nearby village of Cantigny, perched on high ground dominating the countryside. This small village had been recaptured and lost again by French Moroccan forces before it was firmly incorporated into the new German front line.

The initial successes of Ludendorff's "Michael" offensive panicked the Allied High Command. At a meeting at Doullens on the 26th, the British agreed that Gen. Ferdinand Foch be "charged by the British and French governments with the coordination of the action of the Allied armies on the Western Front. ..." This move, along with the earlier creation of Supreme War Council, gave the promise of a more coordinated Allied effort to contain the German offensives, an unintended result from Ludendorff's perspective.

A second result stemming from the German breakthrough was "Black Jack" Pershing's decision (wholeheartedly backed by Secretary of War, Newton D. Baker) to offer AEF divisions to the Allied High Command to plug holes in the line where needed. Specifically, he believed that the Yanks of the U.S. 1st Infantry Division (1st ID), having passed three bitter winter months near Seicheprey along the southern border of the St. Mihiel salient coping with constant shelling, gas attacks and trench raids in muddy, rat-infested trenches, were now ready for real combat. (Over the winter of 1917-18, there were only four American divisions in France, the 1st, 2nd, 26th and 42nd. The latter three were scattered among their training camps around Neufchâteau.) And, by their example, proof that the AEF was also ready for a major, independent offensive role. The French, anticipating that the next phase of Ludendorff's offensive would come against their armies in Champagne, weren't convinced that

American help was needed around Montdidier, but were willing to support a limited attack there by the AEF. (In fact, Ludendorff was already moving his first line divisions from their Picardy salient in preparation for his next offensive (codenamed "Georgette") directed against the British in the Pas-de-Calais.)

Nevertheless, Pershing ordered "The Fighting First" to move across France to take over French positions facing Cantigny with the single purpose of driving the Germans back from the town and the high ground it commanded. This attack was really little more than a demonstration of the AEF's readiness for battle.

The 1st ID's cross-country move was epic. The nearly 40,000 doughboys, their 1,000 wagons and 1,700 animals stretched for 17 miles along the road north to Toul where they entrained for Gisors, northwest of Paris. Fifty-car trains left Toul every hour for three days to move the division and its equipment toward its rendezvous. (The trains stopped twice a day for water and coffee, also allowing the doughboys to relieve themselves by hanging off the boxcar couplings.) At Gisors, the division underwent another round of training, this time for the "open warfare" that Pershing and his staff planned for the AEF to initiate someday. (Gen. Oskar von Hutier's stormtroopers had just illustrated how effective it could be. Unfortunately, the AEF learned little about the tactics inherent to the German successes.) The doughboys completed their three-day march from Gisors to temporary billets west of Cantigny on April 20. Burdened by enormous packs, woolen uniforms and leg wrappings, the Americans trudged through the warm spring nights of April 24-25 from their rear holding positions near Ansauvillers, finally groping their way into new positions just before dawn. The 1st Infantry Brigade (16th and 18th Infantries) held the forward positions with the 2nd Brigade (26th and 28th Infantries) in reserve. Two French divisions, the 45th and the 162nd, flanked the Americans, but were not scheduled to participate in the coming attack.

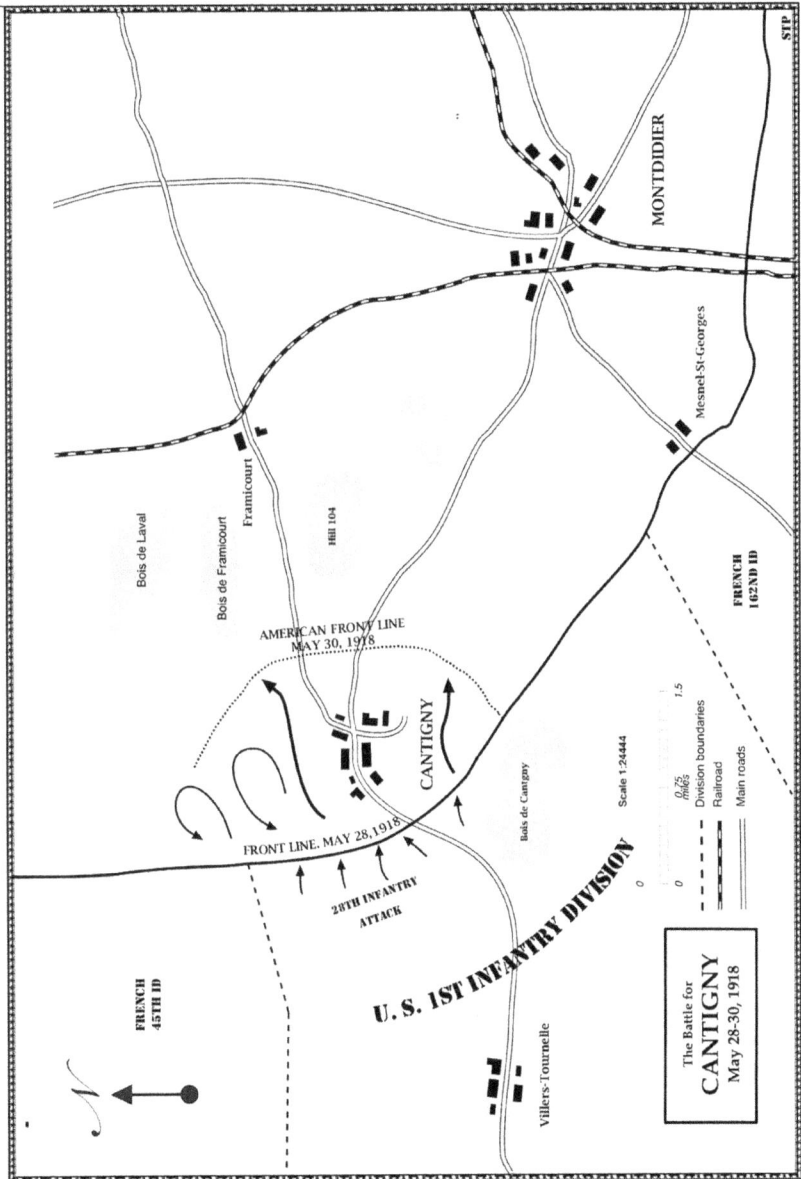

The Battle for
CANTIGNY
May 28-30, 1918

What awaited the 1st ID at Cantigny was pure hell – trench warfare at its worst. Enemy artillery fire was continuous, day or night. German batteries, many out of range of the division's counter-battery fire, dropped 3,400 shells a day (two every minute) on the Big Red One's positions. A low, flat area behind the front line trenches became known as "Death Valley" due to the constant barrage falling on it.

Facing the 1st ID behind their wire were leading elements of the German 82nd Reserve Division consisting of three reserve infantry regiments, the 270th, 271st and 273rd. The 82nd, made up of young recruits, recuperating wounded veterans, overage reserve troops and railway guards, had served earlier on the Eastern Front, but had been largely inactive for the previous two years.

Maj. Gen. Robert L. Bullard (USMA 1885), the 57-year-old West Pointer who Pershing hand-picked to lead the 1st ID, was recuperating from a painful bout with neuritis (he hid his frequent, debilitating attacks all through the war, fearing that Pershing would relieve him if he knew), so the job of working out the details of the Cantigny attack fell largely to his brilliant G-3, Lt. Col. George C. Marshall (VMI, 1901). Marshall opted for surprise. Basically, his "Field Order No. 18" called for the 28th Infantry to spearhead the attack on Cantigny itself, moving quickly on its objective with three battalions abreast and followed by a dozen French tanks and a French flamethrower unit. Maj. Theodore Roosevelt, Jr.'s 1st battalion, 26th Infantry would provide supporting fire, while machine gun companies covered the 28th's flanks and the engineers followed to clear obstacles and establish a new trench line defining the advance.

The short, stocky, Brig. Gen. Charles P. Summerall, Jr. (USMA, 1892) "Sitting Bull" to his men, commanding the division's artillery, designed an artillery support plan that relied heavily on the French, who were to contribute 84 75mm guns, 12 155mm GPF guns and another dozen 220mm mortars. (Unfortunately, just prior to the attack, the French, learning of the German breakthrough on the Chemin des Dames, the third of

Ludendorff's spring offensives, told Summerall that they could only support the Cantigny operation for the first day. Presumably when they pulled out, they made off with a large share of the 200,000 artillery rounds stockpiled for the Cantigny assault.) Summerall's artillery support plan followed closely the German model that had been worked out the year before by Gen. Georg Bruchmüller, who was the reigning German artillery expert – ranging-fire would open at H-1 hour followed by an intense barrage at H-5 minutes. A creeping barrage 1.5 kilometers deep would then protect the infantry as it moved across no-man's-land, through the German positions in Cantigny and beyond.

There was little subtlety in Marshall's plan (other than the complicated artillery support elements), nor did the tactical situation allow for much. Wedged in between French divisions, the Americans had little room for maneuver or for flanking-attacks, other than on a small scale. They were just going to pound the German positions with artillery fire, including gas-shells, and then go straight at them with infantry supported by tanks, flame-thrower squads and flanking machine guns.

Even so, everyone, from Pershing and his GHQ staff to Bullard, Marshall and Col. Hanson Ely, the blunt, acerbic former West Point (1891) football player who commanded the 28th Infantry, was apprehensive. So much rode on the attack's success – the honor of "The Fighting First" representing the AEF and Pershing's insistence on creating an independent American Army under his command topped the list. Bullard and Marshall went so far as to pull the 28th Infantry out of the line so it could stage a mock attack based on models of the battlefield. Marshall, in so far as he could, left nothing to chance, even crawling out into no-man's-land to gauge the terrain himself, knowing that the pending loss of French heavy-artillery support seriously compromised his plan, no matter the currency of his reconnaissance.

Before moving the 1st ID into the front line, Pershing let Bullard know that he would like to address the assembled officers concerning his expectations for the upcoming battle, so at 10:30 in the morning of April 16, Pershing, the "Big Chief" as he was referred to behind his back, stepped from his drab green Locomobile into the courtyard of his HQ château near Chaumont-en-Vexin to address the roughly 900 assembled officers of the "Fighting First." The fifty-seven-year-old Pershing, impeccably attired as always in polished leather cavalry boots and Sam Brown belt, cap pulled down over his eyes, was not an elegant speaker, so his talk was extemporaneous, short and to the point. He expected them, he said, to be flexible and ready to improvise on the battlefield, to take care of their men by setting good examples and by preparing them for the shock of combat. He concluded by saying that he had the greatest confidence that they would be successful in their coming trial and "would make a record of which your country would be proud." What makes this moment in time so memorable for us today is not so much Pershing's words, but rather the remarkable assemblage of officers standing before him. In that group stood a future Vice-President of the United States, a Secretary of State and Army Chief-of-Staff, two other Chiefs-of-Staff, four officers who would later command corps and seven future division commanders. As Matthew Davenport commented in his excellent account, "First Over There" (2015): "It was as if the entire future of the US Army was assembled in the small French courtyard." In a little over a month many of these officers and the men they commanded would be embroiled in a battle as fierce as any American soldiers have ever fought and many would be casualties.

That actual battle for Cantigny began a day ahead of schedule when a *Jagdkommando* team of about 50 attempted a trench raid with the objective of nabbing a Yank or two for intelligence purposes. After a fierce fight, the 50 men of the 3rd Platoon,

Company E, 28th Infantry fought off the attackers, inflicting some 42 casualties. American casualties were high as well – nine killed and another 20 wounded including platoon commander, Lt. Charles Avery, who had been buried alive for three hours by a shell blast. And, the 28th Infantry's main attack on Cantigny was still 24-hours away.

The bulk of the 28th Infantry moved back into its trenches and "funkholes" (doughboy slang for what GIs a generation later would call "foxholes") during the night of May 27-28. The artillery barrage covering its attack began promptly at 04:45 and was promptly answered by German batteries. The fire from American and French guns was intensified at 05:45 as planned, soon silencing the German guns. The men of the first wave, each carrying 220 rounds of rifle ammo, a gas mask and two canteens of water, surged over the top an hour later, their bayonet-tipped rifles at port-arms, sure that the devastating artillery barrage had made their attack a cakewalk. And, for a time it seemed that they were right; in half an hour the 2nd Battalion had moved through Cantigny (or what was left of it, dropping grenades into cellars where the Boche might be hiding) and gone to ground as planned in a semicircle a half-mile east, facing some small wooded areas and a dominant hill (104) still occupied by German infantry. However, attacks on both the northern and southern flanks were not as successful as companies A, K and L were turned back by enemy fire, leaving the rest of the battalion exposed to artillery and flanking machinegun fire. The second and third waves mopped up Cantigny (a team of *poilus* carrying flamethrowers accompanied the third), and then, moved on to reinforce the hasty trench line being established on the open ground to the east. Casualties from long range artillery and machine gun fire mounted during the afternoon including Lt. Col. Robert J. Maxey, the 2nd Battalion commander, leaving Capt. Clarence R. Huebner, now the battalion's senior officer, in command. (A quarter of a century later, Huebner, would command the "Big Red One" on D-Day, when its 16th Infantry landed on Omaha Beach.)

Col. Hanson Ely estimated that by late afternoon a third of his engaged-regiment were casualties.

Gen. von Hutier, the 18th Army commander who had arrived on the battlefield late on the 28th, was satisfied that the American attack was limited and that there was no danger to Montdidier or other German positions, but that assessment did not impede his 82nd Division's efforts to retake Cantigny.

Counterattacks by Boche infantry began in the evening of the 28th and continued through the next two days. Fighting remained intense through the 29th, with Hanson Ely's regiment being steadily worn down by the attacks and a constant rain of artillery shells. (Counter-battery fire was not possible after the French withdrew their heavy artillery.) Ely became almost insubordinate in his frequent demands that his exhausted men be relieved. That relief was in the offing before the German command ordered another futile counterattack at 04:10 on the 30th. This attack consisted of three waves of equally exhausted infantry moving across open ground toward the American salient, covered by fire from their Maxim machine guns. It was crushed by rifle and Hotchkiss machine gun fire from the American trenches. In sending the after-action report back up the chain of command, Ely (or someone at his HQ) noted laconically: "Enemy infantry started across but never reached our lines neither did they return. All quiet now."

Over the night of May 30-31, the 16th Infantry began replacing the 28th in the line, completing the operation on June 1. The AEF's first major test of arms was essentially done with Cantigny firmly in American hands.

From a century's distance, the results obtained from the Cantigny attack do not seem to justify the casualty list. Battles of attrition are usually ugly. Thirty-eight officers and 903 men in the attacking force had either been killed or wounded. Put in another context, the 28th Regiment had lost half of its officers and a third of its men in three days of bitter fighting. Total casualties to all the AEF units involved in the battle reached approximately 1,600. But the attrition didn't end on May 30. By the time the 1st ID was finally pulled out of its Cantigny salient five weeks later, it had suffered another 500 casualties.

The battle effectively destroyed the 82nd German Reserve Division, inflicting about 1,700 casualties, leaving only 2,500 *Soldaten* fit for duty. The difference was that the German Army could not replace its losses during this final stage of the war, but the AEF could, and did. The 28th Infantry was rebuilt in time to fight again in the Allied fall counter-offensives that brought the war to an end.

The most important results of the American victory were undoubtedly its propaganda and morale-boosting effects. The victory was widely reported by the Allied press and cheered by war-weary Europeans. It may have, Matthew Davenport speculates, emboldened Foch to commit the untested U.S. 2nd and 3rd IDs at Château-Thierry three weeks later with decisive results. After the battles at Cantigny, and later around Château-Thierry, no one at Allied High Command HQ could plausibly question the willingness of the half-trained doughboys to fight, but the competence of their officers would continue to raise Allied eyebrows until the end of the war.

Cantigny Memorials:

1st ID Memorial outside Cantigny (1st ID, 1919) off D26
Cantigny American Monument in Cantigny (ABMC, 1937)
Robert R. McCormick Memorial in Cantigny (2005)
28th Infantry (the Black Lion) Memorial in Cantigny (2007)

Cantigny AMBC Memorial

CHÂTEAU-THIERRY: THE REGULARS STAND FAST, MAY-JULY, 1918

Gen. Erich Ludendorff launched his third Spring 1918 Offensive (codenamed "Blücher-Yorck") before dawn on May 27, this time aimed at French and British troops holding forward positions along the Chemin des Dames ridge north of the Aisne River. The French 6th Army commander, Gen. Jacques Duchesne, had apparently learned little in the previous four years of war for he placed his units in forward positions, foregoing a more viable defense-in-depth.

Ludendorff skillfully employed the Hutier/Bruchmüller tactics (short, intense artillery bombardment followed by stormtrooper infiltration) to crush Duchesne's defenses on the Chemin des Dames. German infantry quickly reached the Aisne along a nine-mile front, crossed the river, not halting until they had crossed the Vesle as well, advancing some 13 miles by nightfall. Only the intervention of the French 5th Army on their left flank prevented them from taking Reims, site of one of France's most imposing medieval cathedrals, where her Kings had been crowned since Clovis. (Note: in 1918 the cathedral was in partial ruins having been struck by Heinie shellfire in 1914.)

In three days, the German advance reached the Marne at Château-Thierry, 50 odd miles east of Paris. There it was brought to a halt, partly by battlefield entropy, but largely by the determined stand of two green American infantry divisions thrown into the breach to help stem the French retreat.

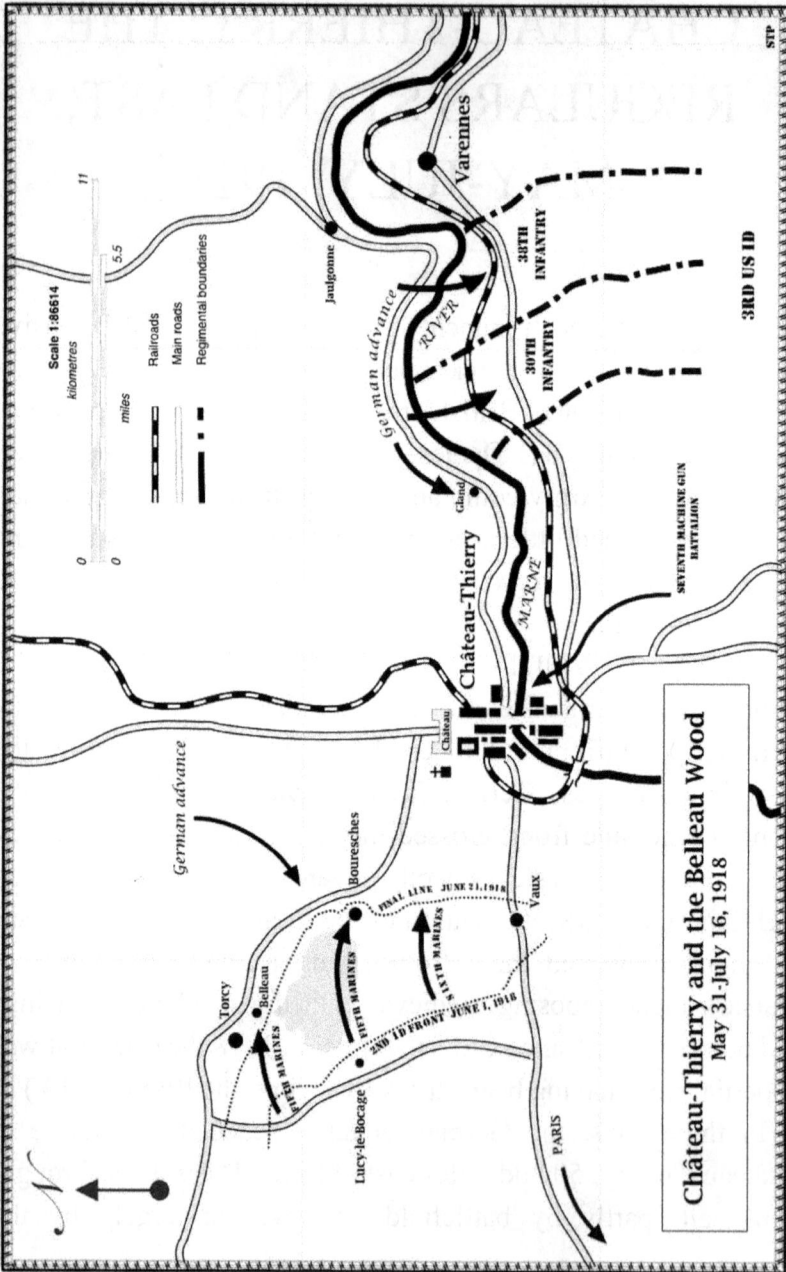

Château-Thierry and the Belleau Wood
May 31–July 16, 1918

Pressure on Pershing to place American troops under French and British tactical command had been mounting all spring; while doing so meant that he had to postpone his long-term plan to create an American field army, he fully understood the gravity of the crisis now facing the Allies. At Generals Foch and Pétain's request he quickly offered to release American divisions – earlier the 1st ID had been sent to Cantigny and now the 2nd and 3rd IDs were rushed in crowded trucks to defend the Marne River line at Château-Thierry. There, they helped halt the German drive on Paris and, in so doing, wrote an indelible chapter in the annals of American military history.

Two companies of the 3rd ID's 7th Machine Gun Battalion, totaling 395 men, were the first Americans to arrive at Condé-en-Brie, just south of Château-Thierry, after a grueling 110-mile, 22-hour ride north in 52 Ford Model T trucks, 6 Ford touring cars and 24 Indian motorcycles, all driven by very inexperienced doughboys and in constant need of repair. At Condé-en-Brie, the trucks expired: "…they took a look at the hill, uttered one or two despairing gasps, and died with their boots on," recalled Maj. John R. Mendenhall (Co. B) who had been along for the ride. After reaching Château-Thierry on foot, the machine gun companies quickly established positions in the town (Co. A on an island in the river, Co. B strung out east to the sugar factory with one section positioned north of the river) covering the two remaining bridges over the Marne taking on all comers. Over the next three days, this determined contingent of Yanks, who were without previous combat experience, successfully fought alongside the French 33rd Colonial Infantry to defend those bridges until they could be blown up.

After failing to force a crossing of the Meuse at Château-Thierry, Kraut forces slid west, occupying the village of Vaux and the nearby Belleau Wood in preparation for a further advance toward Paris. There, they ran headlong into the 2nd ID with its Fourth Marine Brigade that only days before had been placed under the command of Brig. Gen. James G. Harbord, recently Pershing's chief of staff and longtime friend.

The Belleau Wood

Renowned as the stand of the 3rd ID along the Marne would become in American military annals, that fame was initially eclipsed by the actions of the Fourth Marine Brigade in driving the Boche from the miniscule *Bois de Belleau*, a plot of dense woods and rocks that would thenceforth be known as the *Bois de la Brigade de Marine*. When a panicked French officer retreated through the marine position west of the *Bois* around June 2, he suggested they fall back as well. (After all, civilians were already fleeing Paris by the thousands, believing *"la guerre est finie."*) Marine Corps legend has it that Capt. Lloyd Williams, shot back, "Retreat? Hell, we just got here." (Much later, Maj. Frederick M. Wise, commanding the 2nd Battalion, 5th Marines, also claimed to have uttered those words.)

Ordered by French Gen. Joseph Degoutte to take the supposedly lightly-defended, kidney-shaped hunting preserve (about 1000 x 3000 yards), the marines first attacked from the west on June 6 in long 1914-style lines with little or no artillery support, only to be caught in the open by Kraut machine guns. (The recent successes of the new von Hutier "open warfare" tactics had apparently little impact on the marines' badly outdated tactics so favored by Pershing, Harbord and the GHQ staff.) In two attacks across the open ground that day, the Brigade took 1087 casualties, the bloodiest day in Marine Corps history before Tarawa in 1943, another ill-planned operation.

Initially driven to ground by the Maxims, yet struggling on through the difficult terrain, the marines stubbornly persevered for the next three weeks, until at last Maj. Maurice Shearer, commanding the exhausted 3rd Battalion, Fifth Marines, could report that, "Woods now U.S. Marine Corps entirely."

That patch of strategically unimportant real estate cost the Marine Brigade some 5200 casualties (750 dead) or about half its combat strength. That the Boche in the Belleau Wood could have been contained or at least neutralized by artillery and gas misses the point. As historian Edward M. Coffman maintained, the symbolic nature of such costly victories (citing Army of the Potomac stands in the West Wood at Antietam and on Cemetery Ridge at Gettysburg during the American Civil War to illustrate his point) far exceeds its immediate strategic importance. The Belleau Wood had been a German redoubt until the marines wrested it from them, demonstrating the fighting spirit of the AEF and its 2nd ID (the Marine Brigade in particular). Both Allied and German high commands took close note.

(Incidentally, the publicity the Marine Brigade received in the American press for its fight in the Belleau Wood came at the expense of U.S. Army doughboys. It seems that the AEF had forbidden war correspondents from mentioning specific Army units or personnel in the stories they filed, a restriction the marines temporarily escaped due to the misinformed action of one censor. Hence, the embedded journalists focused their attention on the exploits of the marines in the Wood, not mentioning the major participation of equally brave doughboys from the 2nd ID. That "unintended" slight rankled the Regular Army for years.)

Vaux

The sacrifices of the Marine Brigade in the Belleau Wood paid tangible dividends in the 2nd ID's next offensive aimed at driving the Boche from Vaux, a village just west of Hill 204 where the American Château-Thierry Monument stands today. Based on meticulous intelligence estimates gathered by Col. Arthur L. Conger, the division's G-2, and from displaced villagers, aerial photography and night patrols, the 3rd Infantry

Brigade developed an attack plan that made maximum use of the division's available firepower – artillery, automatic rifles, hand and rifle grenades as well as the usual rifle and bayonet. When the attack went in just after 18:00 the evening of July 1, the infantry quickly overran Vaux, and then, established a defensive line that it held against the inevitable German counterattack. The attacking force suffered 328 casualties while inflicting 926 on the enemy.

Marine Corps Memorial in the *Bois de la Brigade de Marine.*

According to historian Mark E. Grotelueschen in his "The AEF Way of War" (2007), the battle was a classic application of the "trench warfare" tactics the division had learned from the

French. Unfortunately, when the division was again committed to battle 17 days later near Soissons, poor planning on the part of the French (the rush to get the division to its start line eliminated any chance of adequate artillery support) and Harbord's insistence on the AEF's outmoded "open warfare" tactics, meant that the division's impressive advance was marred by an excessive number of casualties. Only when Brig. Gen. John A. Lejeune, USMC (USNA, 1888) took command on July 28 was the 2nd ID firmly launched on its path to greatness as the premier combat division in the AEF.

German artillery piece near Belleau Wood.

The "Rainbows" near Reims

While the U.S. 2nd and 3rd IDs were writing *fini* to the German drive toward Paris (since March 23 the city had been under bombardment from German long-range guns located in a forest near Laon and thousands of civilians were fleeing the city), the 42nd ID saw action with the French Fourth Army east of Reims. Forewarned of the time and date of the coming attack (at dawn on July 15), French Gen. Henri Gouraud pulled his troops back from their front line trenches to reestablish a main line of resistance farther east, then, preempted the German attack with an artillery barrage of his own. Even so, some doughboys of the Rainbow Division found themselves fighting off Boche infantry in hand-to-hand combat, suffering about 1750 casualties for their effort, yet they held, helping contain the German salient on its eastern flank.

Rock of the Marne

Meanwhile, the German 10th and 36th Divisions reached the Marne between Chateau-Thierry and Varennes, the sector where French Gen. Jean Degoutte had inserted the U.S. 3rd ID into the defensive line south of the river. Maj. Gen. Joseph T. Dickman, commanding the 3rd, disobeyed Degoutte's orders to reinforce his front line some 300 to 400 yards south of a railroad embankment, opting instead to form his main line of resistance even farther back. Despite a preemptive artillery strike before dawn on July 15, German guns were able to answer with a gas barrage, forcing American infantrymen to fight wearing their awkward gas masks. The two easternmost regiments, the 30th and 38th, took the brunt of the attack. Crossing the Marne in boats and on makeshift bridges, Boche infiltrators were able to gain a foothold on the south bank along the front held by the 30th Infantry. The 30th pulled back leaving the left flank of the 38th open. Since the French to east had also withdrawn, Col. Ulysses Grant McAlexander found his regiment defending the Marne crossing along both sides of a narrow valley. And defend it did. For 14 hours the *Soldaten* and doughboys battled toe-to-toe until the former relinquished the Marne.

Formed only eight months before from the 4th, 7th, 30th and 38th Infantry Regiments (also attached were the 10th, 18th and 76th Field Artillery and the 6th Engineer Regiments) at Camp Greene, N.C., the 3rd ID would henceforth proudly carry the appellation: "The Marne Division." (In 1939, the 38th Infantry was stripped from the 3rd ID and reassigned to the 2nd ID as part of the U.S. Army's divisional downsizing and reorganization. (It fought as part of the 2nd ID throughout WWII, however, the 38th Infantry's shoulder patch continued to bear the inscription "The Rock of the Marne" and the diagonal blue and white stripes of the 3rd ID.)

Ludendorff ordered up two more late spring offensives to straighten his lines between Montdidier and Château-Thierry with limited success. He canceled his final planned attack in Flanders because of lack of resources and manpower. His *Kaiserschlacht* had run its course and with its demise went any realistic hope that Imperial Germany could win the war on the Western Front. The battles at Cantigny, Reims and around Château-Thierry were the turning points, attesting to both the combat abilities and the numbers of doughboys now pouring into France. Still, months of bitter fighting remained before a broken Ludendorff would step down as Quartermaster General, allowing the Imperial War Cabinet to request the Armistice that finally ended the "War to End All Wars."

Château-Thierry Cemetery, Memorials and Markers

3rd U.S. Infantry Division Memorial, Avenue Jules Lefebvre, Château-Thierry

Maison de l'Amitié Franco Américaine, 2 place des États-Unis, Château-Thierry

Demarcation Stones, Château-Thierry

Château-Thierry Monument, west of the city

U.S. Marine Memorial, Belleau Wood, west of the city

Aisne-Marne American Cemetery, west of the city

Massive Château-Thierry Monument, which sustained some World War II damage.

SOISSONS: THE 1ST AND 2ND DIVISIONS ATTACK, JULY 18-21, 1918

The tide of war had turned at last. As the German military machine ground to a halt in July, a month in which another 300,000 plus American soldiers reached France, Foch, Haig and Pershing were preparing to go on the offensive. Their first concern was to eliminate the salients created by the German spring offensives before dealing with the long-existing one to the east of St. Mihiel. Given the disasters of 1917 at Chemin des Dames and Passchendaele, it's a wonder that the Allies had the fortitude to go on the offensive again, but the arrival of all those Yanks did wonders for the morale at Foch's HQ.

A rumor circulated through the 1st ID to the effect that it was about to be rotated back to the U.S. to participate in an upcoming Liberty Bond drive. It is doubtful if many of the veterans of Cantigny put much faith in the rumor, so it probably came as no surprise when they and the equally-tested veterans of the 2nd ID were hastily moved into the line on either side of the 1st Moroccan Division, just southwest of Soissons, about 26 miles north of Château-Thierry. The equally hastily developed plan was for the three divisions to attack across rolling wheat fields cut by ravines until they interdicted the supply route (D1) between the two towns, forcing the German army to evacuate the salient created by its earlier drive to the Marne. The attack was to drive about 7 miles across terrain that the Boche had to defend at all costs. At the same time, French and American divisions would attack north from their positions north of Château-Thierry. This massive counterstroke involved the French Fifth, Sixth, Ninth and Tenth Armies – the 1st and 2nd U.S. Divisions were attached to the XX Corps in French Gen. Charles Mangin's Tenth Army.

Gen. Henri-Philippe Pétain, French Army Group Commander, hoping to surprise the Boche, kept most of his attack plan a secret, even from the Americans who were to execute it. As a result, forward elements of both U.S. divisions stumbled along narrow, muddy roads all during the stormy night of July 17-18, reaching their jump-off lines only minutes before H-Hour, minus their divisional artillery and without having halted to eat a decent meal during the night. The 5th Marines and the 9th Infantry actually double-timed it to their lines of departure, and then, had to continue at the same pace to stay up with the rolling barrages covering their advance. The French did provide some artillery support, air cover and tanks to support the American divisions.

The attack began at 04:35 on the 18th when 216 French guns opened fire on known Boche positions. Gen. Summerall, ever the artilleryman and now commanding the Big Red One, at least saw to that, but thought the fire support provided his division was totally inadequate. The German response was feeble at first, enabling all three divisions to advance about two and a half miles by 07:00. Only the black (Senegalese) *poilus* occupying the ground between them lagged, they were wisely using short rushes to outflank the machine gun nests on their front before eliminating them with fixed-bayonets and large knives. (Later, a junior 1st ID officer wrote that his men had finally learned how to conduct open warfare by observing the Senegalese in action!)

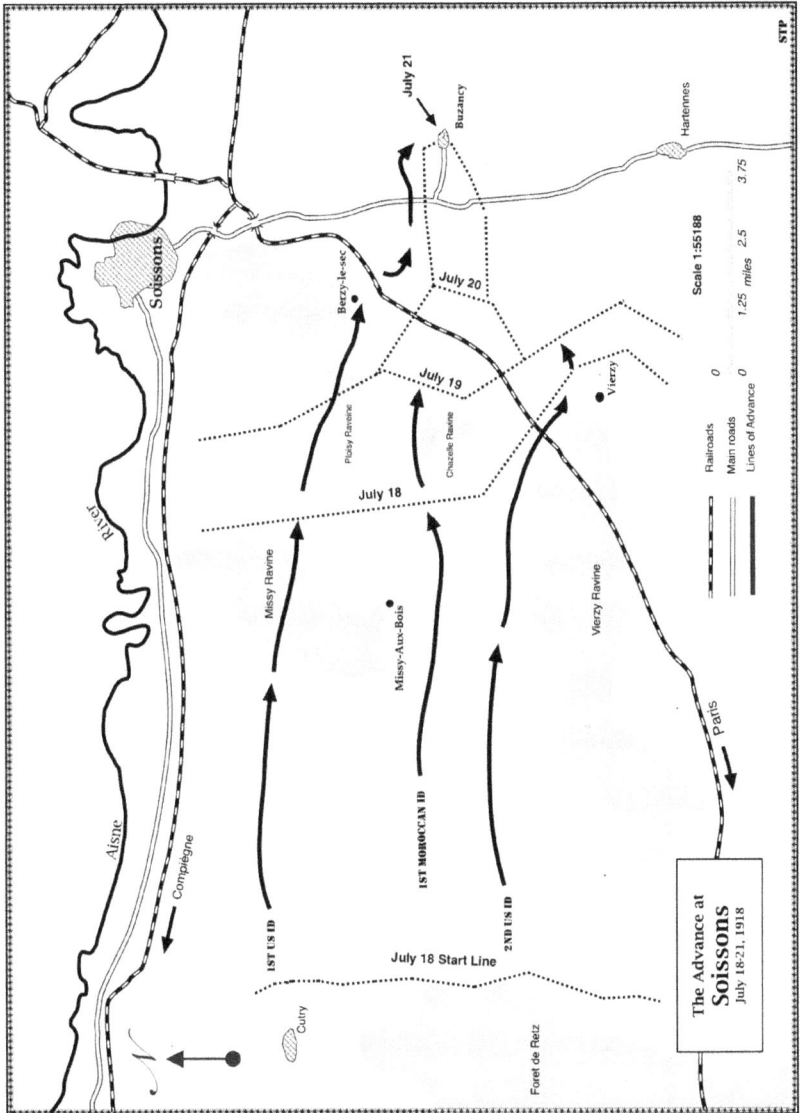

The Advance at
Soissons
July 18-21, 1918

Meanwhile, neither Gen. James Harbord, now in command of the 2nd ID, nor Summerall seems to have learned very much from the Cantigny and Belleau Wood casualty lists. The Yanks attacked in long extended lines across open wheat fields before the Boche Maxims began cutting them down in alarming numbers once they reached the heavily defended ravines – Missy in the case of the 1st ID and Vierzy for the 2nd ID. Both attacks went to ground at that point. Only after a pause, during which Harbord reorganized his regiments, did the exhausted 9th and 23rd Infantries finally overrun the Vierzy ravine, grinding to a halt about five miles from their start lines. During the night the Germans brought up reserves that turned the next day into a bloody one for the attacking doughboys and leathernecks. Harbord, thinking that the Germans were about to crack and urged on by his French superiors, committed his reserve, the 6th Marines, in yet another attack across open fields without artillery support. By the time the attack sputtered to a halt at nightfall over half the regiment were casualties. Obviously James Harbord, who had only commanded the division for four days, had something to prove to his French and American superiors, and did so with the reckless expenditure of his men's lives – the 2nd ID suffered 4,319 casualties in two days of fighting. His impassioned plea for the immediate relief of his weary command comes across as rather hollow today.

It took three more days of hard fighting across more ravines before the 1st ID breached the highway and rail line at Buzancy. After a day's delay, the Big Red One was relieved by the 15th Scottish Division to begin the 11- kilometer hike back to its start line. The attack cost Summerall's division 7,317 casualties, which included 60% of its field-grade officers (all field- grade officers in the 26th Infantry were either dead or in field hospitals). This high price the Allied generals were willing to pay because the repercussions were so far-reaching: forcing Ludendorff to begin the withdrawal of his armies from the Marne salient and canceling his planned Flanders offensive because he was unable replace his losses. The specter of ultimate defeat now reared its ugly head, becoming a very real consideration for the German General Staff, if not for the Kaiser and his entourage tucked away safely in Berlin or Spa.

"Black Jack" Pershing, who held his fighting generals with great affection, soon bumped Harbord up the ladder to command the Services of Supply, and later, Summerall to the command of the V Corps.

The dead and missing from the two infantry divisions are remembered today in the American Aisne-Marne Cemetery.

Soissons Memorials

2nd ID Marker, Vierzy
Buzancy Military Cemetery (British), Buzancy

American doughboys on the attack. (Photo: Wikimedia)

AISNE-MARNE OFFENSIVE: ELIMINATING THE MARNE SALIENT

Gen. Hunter Liggett's I Corps also played a pivotal role in driving the Germans out of the Marne salient starting in July. Earlier there had been some questions about Liggett's fitness for field command because he was badly overweight, but Pershing, overlooking that flaw because of his ability, gave him command of his I Corps consisting of the U.S. 26th and the French 167th infantry divisions. The 3rd, 4th, 28th, 32nd, 42nd and 77th IDs also fought in the Allied push from the Marne River north to the Vesle that finally bogged down before the Vesle in early August.

During that drive north the 167th and 168th IRs (Alabama and Iowa National Guards comprising the 84th Brigade of the 42nd "Rainbow" Division) fought a memorable action at Croix Rouge Farm northeast of Château-Thierry. Ordered forward without artillery support on a rainy, late July 26 afternoon, two battalions of the Alabamians stormed across the 800 yards of open ground around the farmhouse, through carefully prepared Boche machine gun and infantry positions, often fighting hand-to-hand, to capture the farm. In the attack on the farmhouse itself, the 2nd Battalion of the Iowans rushed the fortified complex in support of the 3rd Alabama battalion, taking heavy casualties. It likewise proved a costly day for the entire 167th IR; the charge left it with 162 dead and hundreds more wounded. Boche losses were estimated at 283 *Soldaten*.

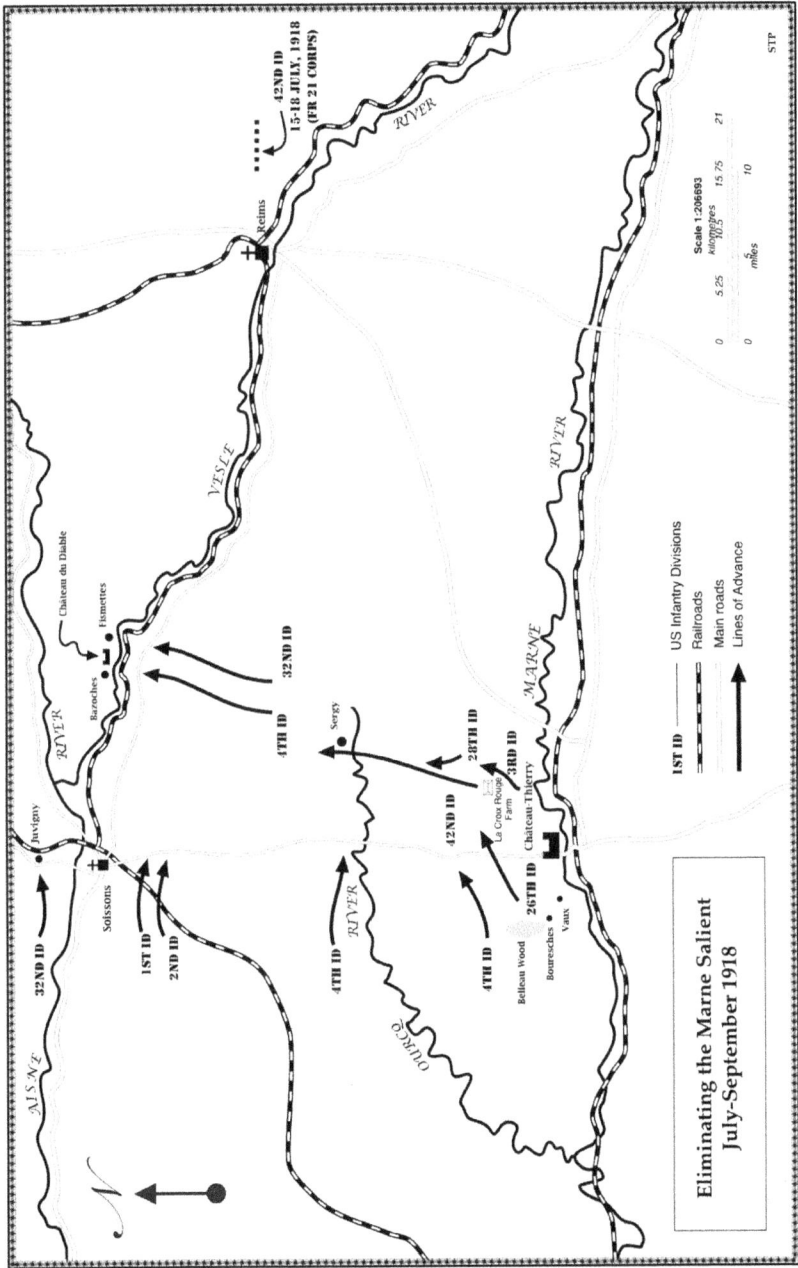

Eliminating the Marne Salient
July–September 1918

1ST ID ——— US Infantry Divisions
Railroads
Main roads
Lines of Advance

42ND ID
15-18 JULY, 1918
(FR 21 CORPS)

Reims

VESLE RIVER

Chateau du Diable
Hismettes
Bazoches

32ND ID
4TH ID

Sergy

28TH ID
42ND ID
La Croix Rouge Farm
3RD ID
Chateau-Thierry

26TH ID
Belleau Wood
Bouresches
Vaux
4TH ID

MARNE RIVER

AISNE
RIVER
Juvigny
Soissons
32ND ID
1ST ID
2ND ID
4TH ID
OURCQ RIVER

Scale 1:206693
kilometres
0   5.25   10.5   15.75   21
0   5   10
miles

STP

Despite its losses, the Rainbows continued their attack, driving the Boche behind the Ourcq River, about 12 miles north of the Croix Rouge Farm, before being relieved by two regiments of the 4th ID. During the week of fighting that began at the Farm, the division lost 5,529 doughboys – 945 were killed outright, 269 died later of wounds. The 167th IR alone lost 55 percent of its combat strength. Brig. Gen. Douglas MacArthur (USMA, 1903), who briefly commanded the 84th Brigade before taking over the division, later wrote that, "for its gallantry" the fight for the Croix Rouge Farm "has not been surpassed in military history."

As the Allied advance pushed north, the 28th and the 77th IDs, now in the front line, were ordered to hold exposed positions in the Vesle River valley, "Death Valley" to the men hunkered down in their funkholes, until the Germans fell back a short distance to the Aisne where again they dug in. There, the stalemate continued until late September, when the final Allied offensive commenced on multiple fronts.

German units also took heavy casualties in their retreat from the Marne, forcing the break-up of ten divisions to provide replacements for depleted front-line units, but panic had not yet set in. American commanders chafed under the command of Gen. Degoutte, and French officers in general, complaining that their orders were often confusing, late and wasteful of American lives, but they kept up the pressure on the methodically retreating Germans until they were relieved and regrouped as part of the First American Army that was poised to attack in the American commanded Meuse-Argonne offensive in late September.

Memorials

Croix Rouge Farm Memorial
Oise-Aisne ABMC Cemetery

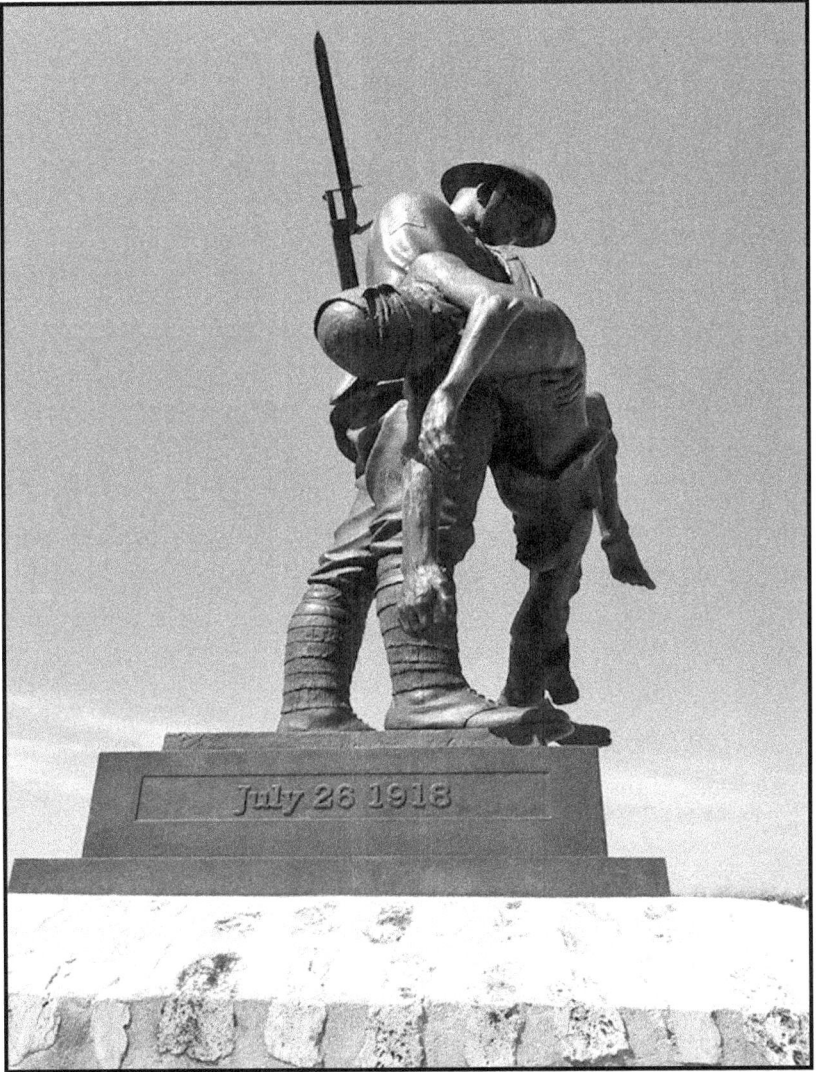

Evocative statue, dedicated to the 167th Alabama Regiment, at Croix Rouge Farm.

Renowned poet Joyce Kilmer lies with more than 6,000 others at Oise-Aisne Cemetery.

LE HAMEL AND THE ST. QUENTIN CANAL: FIGHTING WITH THE DIGGERS, SEPTEMBER-OCTOBER 1918

Despite his best laid plans and often stated intentions, Pershing was never able to collect all the doughboys arriving in France into the powerful American Army that he envisioned under his command. The demands for American manpower were unrelenting and inevitably units, as large as divisions, slipped from "Black Jack's" control. Two divisions, the 27th and 30th (II Corps) served with the "Diggers" (as Australian infantrymen were nicknamed) during the counter-offensive in September and October 1918 and their dead are remembered by a memorial and a cemetery north of St. Quentín. Their story is as much one of bravery and perseverance as any in the AEF.

Beginning in April 1918, ten American divisions began their trench warfare training with the British, but only five actually remained under Field Marshal Douglas Haig's command for the long term. When Pershing set out to create his First Army, he wanted all the divisions back. In the testy compromise that resulted, an unhappy Haig was allowed to keep only two divisions, the 27th and 30th; later, during the Meuse-Argonne meat grinder, "Black Jack" came to regret that compromise.

After training with the British, the U.S. II Corps, under the command of Maj. Gen. George W. Read (USMA, 1883), found itself attached to Lt. Gen. Sir John Monash's Australian Corps where it felt very much at home. Monash, a Jewish civil engineer, was obviously not your typical British Army general officer, but he enjoys the reputation today of being among the most competent officers, protective of his "Diggers" and doughboys, and an innovative tactician. After his successful battle at Amiens in August 1918, King George V knighted him on the battlefield, the first British commander so honored in 200 years. Gen. Read probably considered himself fortunate to have his corps placed under Monash's command.

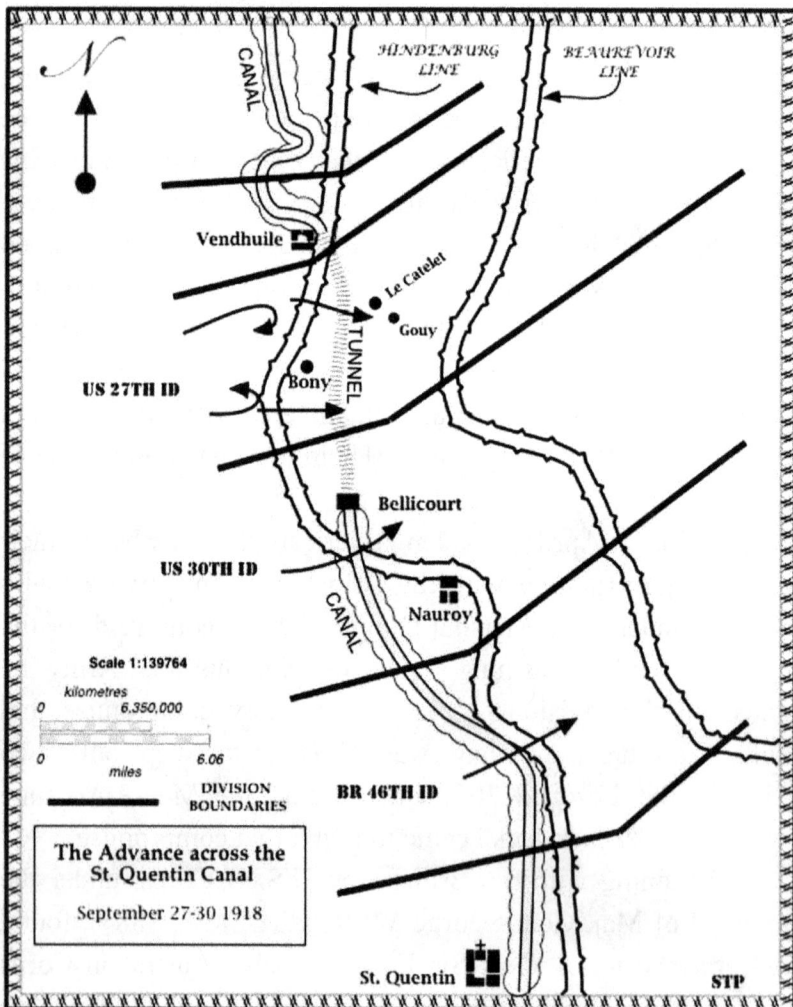

The Advance across the
St. Quentin Canal

September 27-30 1918

The first real action of the doughboys with the "Diggers" came at Le Hamel ridge just south of the Somme. In light of the battles that followed, the attack at Le Hamel was on a very small scale; its objective was to drive the Boche off the ridge, back some mile and a half, using a combined infantry/armor attack. The Australians provided the bulk of the force, eight battalions, while the U.S. 33rd ID (Illinois National Guard), not yet transferred to the U.S. First Army, contributed eight rifle companies. Sixty tanks provided close support for the infantry; Monash even provided for pinpoint airdrops of ammunition and supplies to his advancing troops.

The attack was set to jump off at dawn on July 4, but that was before Pershing learned of it during an inspection tour, he ordered the doughboys withdrawn. Monash balked at Pershing's demands, telling Haig – no Americans, no attack. Haig backed his corps commander and the attack went in as scheduled with the thousand or so doughboys performing well. American losses came to 176 officers and men. Cpl. Thomas A. Pope won the Medal of Honor for taking out a machine gun nest single-handedly with a bayonet charge. Pershing was furious, perceiving the entire incident as part of an underhanded British effort to use American units without prior approval from his headquarters. In the ensuing shuffle, he removed all but two National Guard divisions, the 27th (New York) and the 30th (Tennessee, the Carolinas and Georgia) from direct British control; they remained with Monash's Australian Corps in the British 4th Army. Two months later, those two divisions became key units in the British plan to attack the Hindenburg Line north of St. Quentín.

Typical of Monash, he planned this September attack, part of Foch's general counter-offensive along the Western Front, with meticulous care and attention to detail. He believed that if his plan was thoroughly understood and executed exactly it would succeed. But, the attack of his corps along the St. Quentín canal and tunnel is a textbook lesson on the limitations of his approach and a validation of Helmuth von Moltke's adage that no military plan survives contact with the enemy. No amount of meticulous planning could compensate for the greenness of the untrained Yanks Monash was about to throw into the cauldron of battle.

The Boche had placed this section of the *Kriemhilde Stellung* behind the St. Quentín canal and tunnel, public works (dating from the time of Napoléon Bonaparte) completed a century before. Monash's attack plan called for his two American divisions to attack over the tunnel section, a relatively featureless 3.5-mile front – farmland that encompassed the villages of Bellicourt, Bony and Gouy. The British 46th Division (North Midland), specially outfitted with bridging equipment, was scheduled to attack to the south where the canal ran above ground. Other units of the British Army, not belonging to Monash's corps, would be attacking in the north.

Monash's plan was straightforward and explained in detail to the American commanders — the two American divisions would jump off in a dawn attack, preceded by massive artillery preparation that included mustard gas and they were to be accompanied by tanks that would carry them across the main trench line and through the support trenches. Once the *Stellung* had been breached, Monash's two Digger divisions would pass through the Yanks to exploit the breakthrough.

Despite all the careful preparation, the Aussie's plan unraveled before it could be implemented. The trouble began when a British division holding the line failed to gain control of the start-line for the 27th ID, which meant that at dawn on September 27, the 106th Infantry had to put in an attack without much artillery preparation. Three times the doughboys overran Kraut defensive positions, only to be pushed back each time. The failure to take the start line cascaded back into the attack plans for the 29th, upsetting all the carefully prepared artillery schedules. The division commander, a 44-year-old National

Guardsman, Gen. John F. O'Ryan (NYU law degree, 1898), requested a postponement and, to his credit, Monash seconded the request, only to have it turned down at Army level by Lt. Gen. Henry Rawlinson, commander of the Fourth Army, who, along with Haig, had perpetrated the British disaster at the Somme two years before. Haig and Rawlinson's great 1918 counter-offensive of personal vindication was not going to be delayed by one American National Guard Division's inability to take and hold ground; it would have to suffer the consequences of its failure in order that the Fourth Army attack remained coordinated with the entire Allied effort. (Rawlinson's decision must be kept in mind when appraising Pershing's ongoing, sometimes nasty fight to keep American units out of foreign hands.)

And, suffer it did. In the follow up fighting that took place on September 29, day-one of the main assault, the 107th Infantry took a thousand casualties, 50 percent of its fighting strength, arguably the greatest loss by any American regiment during one day's fighting in the war. Many Yanks, wounded or just holed up, were left in no-man's-land, hopefully to be rescued later.

Given the difficulties on the 27th, when the main attack jumped off at dawn on the 29th the doughboys of the II Corps had a surprisingly easy time of it. The 30th ID had its advance eased by the success of the British 46th Division in forcing the canal, thus covering its right flank.

Not long after messages arrived at Monash's HQ of the American successes in reaching their objectives, word began to trickle in from the follow up Australian divisions that their advance was running into considerable resistance from Kraut infantry, *Soldaten* they figured the inexperienced Americans had not paused to mop up. The truth was more fascinating and complex. The wily Bosch had hidden in the tunnel, allowing the Yanks to move beyond the trench line on the farther bank, before popping up from underground to engage them from the rear. It fell to the Australians to clean up the mess, but even they were unable to do much in the 27th ID's zone. It wasn't until the 31st that the Corps' first day's objectives were finally reached.

Read's corps was given a week to recuperate, during which it received no replacements, before being pressed back into service. Both divisions fought to the Selle River, paused, and then forced the river on October 17th. Three days later, Rawlinson pulled them out of the line and their war was over.

Since the beginning of the offensive 24 days before, II Corps had taken 13,182 casualties. Yanks of the 30th ID would eventually have a dozen Medals of Honor conferred on them, the largest number for any division in the AEF. Gen. Monash later wrote that the doughboys were very brave, but not well trained. He should have known since their training had been his responsibility for months before the attack across the St. Quentin Canal.

Cemetery and Memorials

Australian Corps Memorial, Le Hamel
Somme American Cemetery, Bony
Bellicourt American Monument, Bellicourt

SAINT MIHIEL: PRELUDE TO VICTORY, SEPTEMBER 12-13, 1918

Pershing finally won his battle to create an independent American Army in early May when he secured agreement from the Allied commanders. That agreement became a reality on July 10 when Foch said, "To-day, when there are a million Americans in France, I am going to be still more American than any of you. . . . The American Army must become an accomplished fact." By the end of the month, an American field army consisting of two corps (I – Maj. Gen. Hunter Liggett (USMA, 1879), and III – Maj. Gen. Robert L. Bullard) was operational. French Premier Georges Clemenceau congratulated Pershing: "History awaits you. You will not fail it." (Quotations from Edward M. Coffman, "The War to End All Wars," p. 263.)

Pershing's long-time objective for his new command was the reduction of St. Mihiel salient, a piece of French real estate between the Moselle and the Meuse Rivers that the Germans had held since 1914. It was considered a "quiet" sector of the front where several American divisions had gained their first experience of trench warfare. Now, it was about to become very active.

This was no small operation. Pershing now had four corps (eight and a half American divisions combined with four French in the I and IV Corps) for the main attack from the south. Another French corps was assigned for a follow-up attack, while the American V Corps (two divisions plus a brigade) was readied for a secondary attack from the northwest. The Germans were defending the salient with eight depleted divisions and a brigade.

The planning for this offensive was a formidable task that fell largely to four junior American staff officers: Fox Conner, Hugh A. Drum, Walter S. Grant and George C. Marshall. They and their staffs had three weeks to plan for the night movement of 500,000 doughboys and 110,000 *poilus* with their 200,000 tons of supplies and nearly 3,000 cannon (plus 50,000 tons of ammunition) to the jump-off lines without alerting the enemy. In the middle of this operation, Foch and Pétain maneuvered Pershing into agreeing to a major change in the strategic plan for the follow-up offensive.

Now, instead of striking north along the Moselle valley toward Metz, the logical extension of the St. Mihiel attack and a potential war-ending blow against German logistics, the Americans were to be moved north where they would be inserted in the Allied line between the Meuse River and the Argonne Forest, anchoring the right wing of a general Allied offensive across northern France. This new plan, the brainchild of Field Marshal Sir Douglas Haig, commander of the British forces, was enthusiastically supported by Marshal Foch, who then maneuvered Pershing into accepting it as the price for his First Army command. Divisions were realigned, a secondary attack temporarily canceled, which generated considerable rancor, and a preparatory artillery barrage vetoed, then reinstated, before the attack kicked off at dawn on a rainy September 12.

Gen. William "Billy" Mitchell's Army Air Service put over 900 airplanes in the air to cover the attack. Fortunately for the doughboys involved, the Boche defenders had already decided to withdraw from the salient, hence they were caught in some disarray although the actual withdrawal had not yet begun.

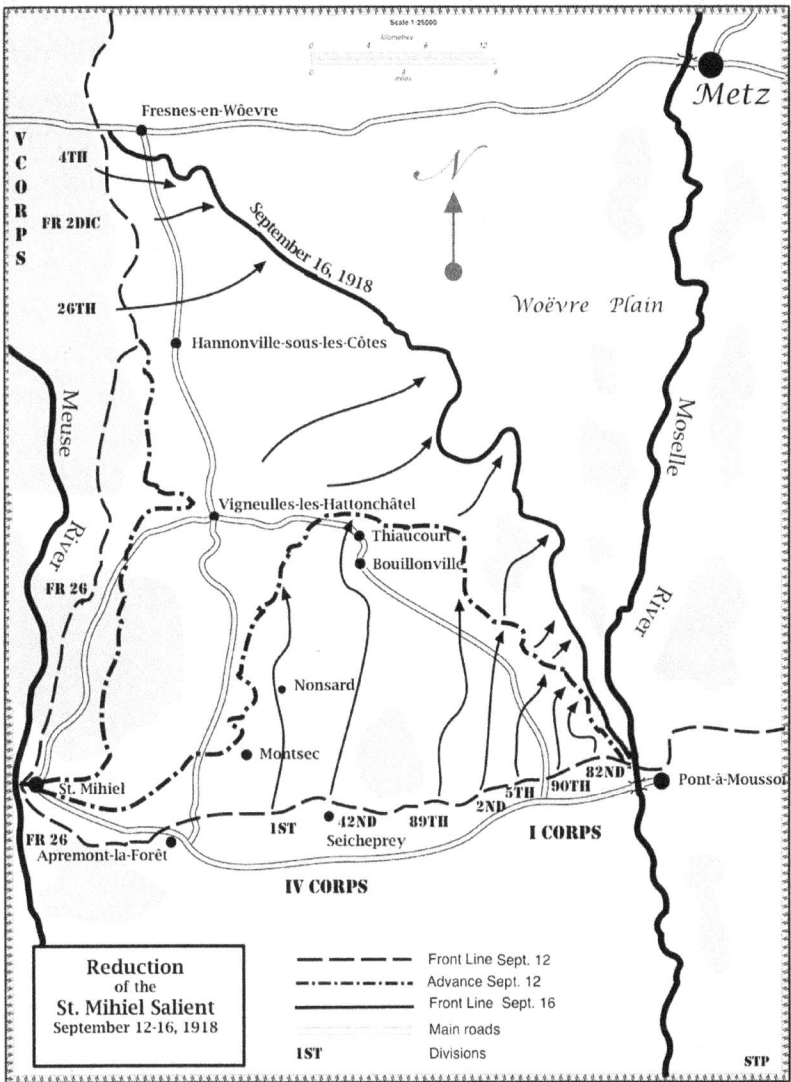

Reduction of the St. Mihiel Salient
September 12-16, 1918

– – – –	Front Line Sept. 12
–··–··–	Advance Sept. 12
———	Front Line Sept. 16
	Main roads
1ST	Divisions

The attack went well from the start, aided somewhat by a clever deception plan that sucked off three German divisions to defend against a possible attack through the Belfort gap far to the south. Allied artillery batteries began firing continuously at 01:00. Along the southern front, the 1st and 42nd IDs made good progress against the retreating enemy. At the far eastern edge of that line, the 90th ID (Texas and Oklahoma National Guards) had slower going, although many *Soldaten* they encountered preferred surrender to continuing the fight. Even troops of the 2nd Cavalry Division got into the act, probing ahead of the infantry before dismounting to take on machine gun nests. The 2nd and 89th IDs drove quickly north to the town of Thiaucourt on the Rupt de Mad River. The fighting was largely over by the morning of the 13th when the Yanks from the Big Red One met the real Yanks from the 26th ID (the Yankee Division, created in 1917 from New England National Guard units) near Vigneulles, cutting the salient in half, thus allowing Pershing to escort Gen. Pétain into the village of St. Mihiel on "Black Jack's" 58th birthday.

Massive Montsec American Monument at St. Mihiel (Photo: Wikimedia)

Pershing's First Army suffered 7,000 casualties, while the Kraut defenders lost 17,000 men from all causes (2,300 killed and wounded). The road was now open for an attack on Metz and the rail line passing through the Briey-Longwy mining and industrial complex. Instead of taking it, the U. S. First Army now began its move north toward what would become its final, pivotal battle on the Western Front, the Meuse-Argonne Offensive.

Cemetery and Memorials

St. Mihiel American Cemetery
Montsec American Monument
5th ID steles (2)

MEUSE-ARGONNE: THE DECISIVE BATTLE, SEPTEMBER 25 - NOVEMBER 11, 1918

Instead of quickly realigning itself after the collapse of the St. Mihiel salient for a drive toward Metz, a logical move that GHQ had long anticipated, the First Army now began to play its assigned part in the Foch/Haig general offensive that involved a convoluted movement north to fight in the broken country between the Meuse River and the Argonne Forest. It would be challenging to find a more difficult terrain in France for the Americans to fight through, but it was key to the Devil's bargain Pershing made with Foch for the creation of the First U.S. Army.

The Meuse-Argonne battlefield was bordered on the east by the Meuse River, too deep to be forded and which high ground along its east bank provided the defenders with excellent artillery positions. Almost twenty-five miles to the west, the Argonne Forest was a north-south expanse of trees and rocky ravines, with only three primitive forest-roads to support the American offensive. Making any advance through this area even more difficult, German engineers had constructed a number of defensive lines between the Meuse and the Argonne, all named after Wagnerian witches, all formidable. The first day's advance for the Yanks would have to be around and over Montfaucon, a heavily fortified butte that anchored the first line, the Giselher Stellung. Five miles to the north the Boche had constructed an even stronger line, then, in another five miles the doughboys would reach the Kriemhilde Stellung (Hindenburg Line to the Americans), which, in the First Army sector, ran from the Meuse across the northern end of the Argonne to the village of Grandpré. Col. Hugh Drum, First Army chief of staff, whose subordinates drew up Field Order #20 for the attack, later termed the ground as "the most ideal defensive terrain I have ever seen or read about."

The ultimate objective of the Americans in the Meuse-Argonne campaign was a rail line, some 50 miles to the north, which ran through Mézières and Sedan. Interdicting that line, the Allied High Command believed, would break the supply line to the German armies in Belgium and France, causing the Imperial Government to sue for peace before its army was forced to surrender.

The First Army's offensive was not an isolated move — Allied armies were to go on the attack from Lorraine to Flanders, pressuring the Germans everywhere. There were so many American divisions now arriving in France that it was possible for Pershing to allow a number of them to reinforce French and British Armies far from the Meuse-Argonne battlefield.

AEF Units on Detached Duty

Below is a list of other American units that were not parts of the U.S First or Second Armies during the Meuse-Argonne Campaign.

- Four infantry regiments of African-American-Americans (369th, 370th, 371st and 372nd) served with the French Army where they were accepted, performed well and highly decorated.

- The 332nd Infantry ended up in Italy fighting the Austrians.
- The 2nd and 36th IDs fought with the French Fourth Army in Champagne.
- The 91st and 37th IDs fought with the French in Belgium.
- Elements of the 339th Infantry served with other Allied troops around Archangel.
- The 27th and 30th IDs served with the Australian Corps in Picardy.

Another 9,000 Americans spent the winter of 1918-19 in Siberia under the command of Maj. Gen. William S. Graves, attempting to remain neutral in the nasty Russian civil war that was raging.

Field Order #20 outlined overly ambitious goals for the first day's attack – the German forward defensive line, Montfaucon and the second defensive line were to fall on the first day. The formidable *Kriemhilde Stellung* would be overrun on the morning of the second. This optimism was rooted in intelligence reports that indicated that only five under-strength enemy divisions held these intrinsically strong positions. The staff at GHQ believed that a massive bombardment followed by a fast moving advance, coupled with the German Army's lack of reserves, could punch open the way to Sedan in just two days. That turned out to be rather fanciful planning given the terrain, the inexperienced Yank divisions and those formidable German defenses years in the making.

To accomplish this breakthrough, Pershing organized his divisions into three corps – hundreds of thousands of doughboys, many of them draftees who had been in uniform less than four months, thousands of whom had never fired a rifle or been near a combat zone; he positioned them neatly on the ground in an east-west line running through Malancourt.

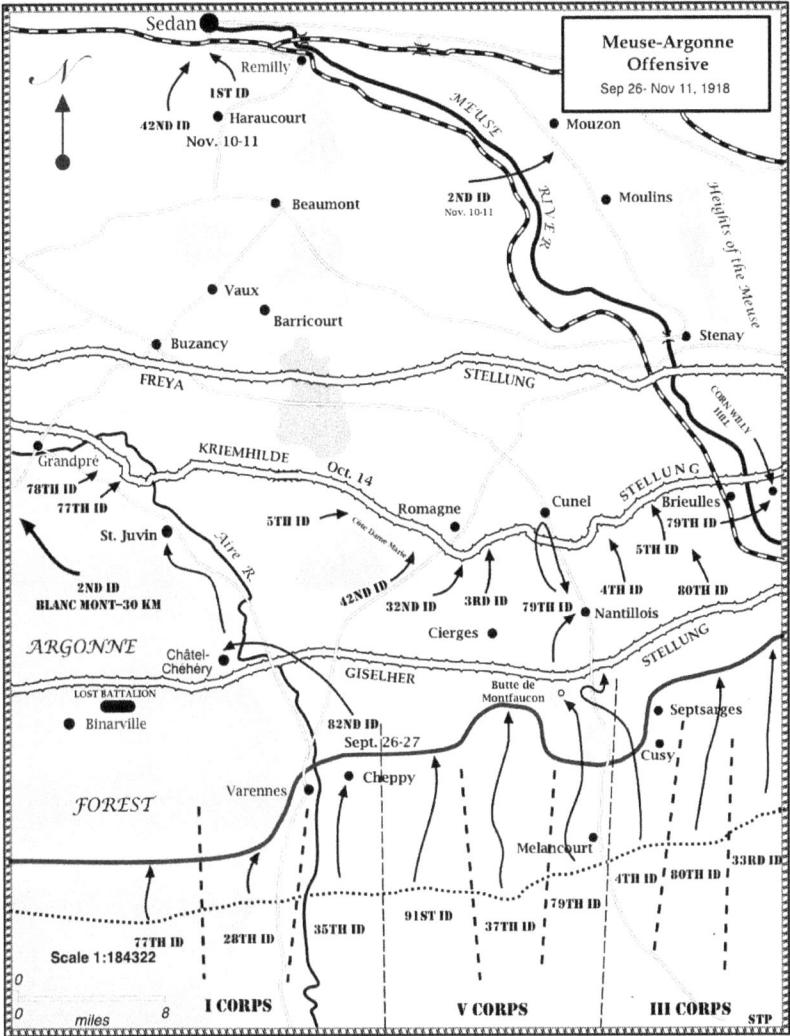

Meuse-Argonne Offensive
Sep 26- Nov 11, 1918

However, before the First Army's attack could kick off, it had to be moved from its location in the St. Mihiel salient 40 or so kilometers north to its start line west of Verdun. Drum assigned his formidable task to Lt. Col. George C. Marshall, who was undaunted. Marshall had only three roads over which to move 600,000 men and their equipment in two weeks. Complicating this movement were the 222,000 French *poilus* scheduled to be evacuated from the area at the same time along the same roads. Making these tasks even more difficult, the relief was to be undertaken at night to maintain the element of surprise. Marshall solved his problems by using one road for motor transport and the other two for horses and foot traffic (*poilus* and doughboys staggering along in columns, groaning under their heavy packs and weapons). The German defenders learned of this massive movement (they could hardly have missed it), but didn't have an inkling as to its size or intended purpose.

When the troop movement ended, the First Army was arrayed with Robert L. Bullard's III Corps to the east, Hunter Liggett's I Corps to the west and George H. Cameron's V Corps in the center, each with three attack divisions forward. Another 14 divisions waited in reserve. From left (west) to right (east), the nine divisions lined up abreast as follows: 77th, 28th, 35th, 91st, 37th, 79th, 4th, 80th, and 33rd. Some were battle-tested, others green, never having experienced combat. Even the battle-tested were often filled with raw recruits. They were largely chosen because of their availability; they could be more easily moved into their start positions than the more experienced divisions that had fought in the St. Mihiel salient. No matter, it was a mighty host.

The preliminary bombardment of the German forward positions began at 23:30 on September 25, when the First Army's big guns opened up on the German rear areas. Then, at 02:30, all the smaller pieces joined in and the 2,700 guns kept at it until 05:30, the designated H-hour. At that time, under a rolling barrage, the infantry rose from the ground and began to move forward through the fog and smoke. At least it wasn't raining. Initially, all seemed to go well, although early on a glitch developed in the advance of the untested 79th ID when its lead-regiments failed to overrun Montfaucon, the key defensive position on their front, in fact, the entire battlefield. Atop the butte, the Boche had cleverly built a tower equipped with a range-finding device that gave them the ability to control artillery fire across the entire 20-mile American front, from the heights of the Meuse to the Argonne Forest. To protect this key post, Montfaucon was heavily reinforced and stubbornly defended once the attack began.

The 79th ID was a National Army division comprised mainly of men from Maryland and Pennsylvania. Before it was shipped to France in 1918, it had been used as a training division, which meant that as soon as cadres of recruits had received some basic training they were stripped from the division and reassigned elsewhere. When Gen. Joseph E. Kuhn's 79th was rushed to the front to take part in the opening assault of the Meuse-Argonne offensive, it was one of the more poorly trained and least experienced units in the AEF. The 79th's ranks, although filled with green recruits, was given the imposing task of storming Montfaucon, nicknamed "Little Gibraltar" because of its defensive strength. Historian William T. Walker, in his recent monograph, "Betrayal at Little Gibraltar" (2016), argues that the original attack plan called for the 79th to attack the butte frontally while a more combat-hardened brigade from the 4th ID would attack its right flank. According to Walker, because of personal ambition and intra-service rivalry, Gen. Robert Lee Bullard, III Corps commander, canceled the flanking attack, instead ordering the 4th to continue its drive north leaving the 79th's regiments to struggle up the rocky slopes of Montfaucon alone, stumbling into two carefully prepared Boche defensive traps. No wonder the division's initial assault on the citadel failed. Nevertheless, the 79th took the butte the following day, and its 316th Infantry actually penetrated the Hindenburg Line west of Cunel on the 29th before being pulled back.

Impressive as Bullard's III Corps' gains were on the first day, the First Army's attack had failed, bogged down everywhere without the dramatic breakthrough that Pershing and his staff optimistically expected. The German Army Group Commander, Gen. Max von Gallwitz, rushed all the troops he could find to plug the front, mixing units where necessary. The American offensive now became a hard, yard-by-yard slog against stubborn resistance by German *Soldaten* fighting in a war they knew was lost, with casualties on both sides mounting every hour. A month would pass before the AEF's second day's objective, the Kriemhilde Stellung, was finally breached.

The 35th ID was an unfortunate exception in that slow, painful advance. The division consisted of the National Guards of Kansas, Missouri and Nebraska (Capt. Harry S. Truman of Missouri commanded its Battery D, 129th Field Artillery Regiment). Friction between Regular Army and National Guard officers had led to the ill-advised removal of the latter just days before the offensive kicked off. The division, with its cohesiveness damaged, now confronted the First Guards Division, one of the best Boche outfits facing the Americans. Despite support from Lt. Col. George S. Patton's light tank brigade, but without effective leadership from its commander, Brig. Gen. Peter E. Traub, and other senior Regular Army officers, the results were predictable. The 35th soon disintegrated into chaos, suffering somewhere between 6,000 and 8,000 casualties before the 1st ID relieved it on October 1. The war, if not the controversy, was over for the 35th ID.

Just prior to the beginning of the Allied offensive, Gen. Pétain made an urgent request for Pershing to release an experienced division to bolster the strength of his Fourth Army scheduled to attack west of the Argonne Forest. "Black Jack" chose the 2nd ID for the job. The division, still commanded by marine Gen. Lejeune, was bivouacked at Toul reorganizing after the St. Mihiel operation. Now part of Charles Summerall's V Corps, Lejeune' unorthodox ideas about employing trench warfare tactics in carefully-planned attacks was supported by his immediate commander. The artillery support plan devised by

Lejeune and his artillery commander was as successful as it was intricate. By October 2, the division had completed the relief of the French 61st Division and was poised to attack Blanc Mont, a heavily fortified hill feature, along a two-mile front. The 4th Marine Brigade (5th and 6th Marines) spearheaded the attack that jumped off the next day at 05:30. Preceded by an intense five-minute artillery barrage, then, followed by a rolling barrage supported by French light tanks, the marines shoved the Boche off the ridge in three hours of tough combat. Gen. Gouraud was so impressed that he called up a French cavalry division in hopes of exploiting the breakthrough, but the German XII Corps quickly reinforced its lines and for the next week the marines and doughboys fought for every yard of ground. (The cavalry, one assumes, went back to its bivouac area to wait for a more propitious day.) Subsequent attacks added another 5,000 casualties to the division's growing list, mostly taken when flanking French divisions left the Yanks' salient exposed, a tally already in excess of 10,000 and there were still to be many more added.

A week later, on the Oct. 10, the Lone Star ID relieved the 2nd; by then, the German Army was in full retreat toward its new positions on the Aisne River.

Long before Oct. 1 the First Army's offensive had stalled far short of its objectives, a fact that Pershing's alibis could not hide from Foch and Clemenceau who were quick to point to the successes of the other Allied Armies to the north. The ensuing pause lasted until fresh Regular Army divisions could be moved to the front to replace those in the initial attack, now worn down from a week of bitter fighting and the devastating effects of the Spanish flu.

The renewed attack began at dawn on October 4 and continued through the next day. Again, gains were limited except for those of the 82nd ID, whose flanking attack behind the German front in the Argonne Forest enabled the relief of the famous "Lost Battalion" and forced the Boche to evacuate their Argonne position.

German trench near "Lost Battalion" site.

To the east, after a week of hard fighting, attacks by the French XVII Corps, aided by the 33rd ID and the 58th Brigade of the 29th ID, had cleared the enemy from the hills east of the Meuse where their artillery had been targeting American infantry. The continuous fighting since September had used up the 33rd ID, which had suffered more gas casualties than any other American division – in excess of 2,000 – so Pershing withdrew it from the line in late October.

Yet another attack on the *Kriemhilde Stellung* opened on October 10 with the advance of the 32nd ID on a ridge known as the Côte Dame Marie, near Romagne. Pershing hoped that the 32nd's attack would pin down the defenders enabling the 42nd and 5th IDs to capture the ridge in a pincer movement. The fight went on for three days without much success before Capt. Edward B. Strom of the 3rd Battalion, 127th Infantry was sent forward with seven men to knock out a machine gun nest covering a gap in the German wire. Strom and his men managed to crawl close enough to attack the nest with rifle grenades before charging it. In the ensuing fight, the doughboys captured ten machine guns and took 15 prisoners without losing a man. Without those guns to stop the ensuing American attack, the Boche abandoned the Côte Dame Marie. The *Kriemhilde Stellung*, the last of the formidable defensive lines in the Meuse-Argonne, was breached at last.

In the fight for the Côte Dame Marie, Lt. Samuel Woodfill of the 60th Infantry (5th ID) fought a one-man battle that matched the better known exploits of Cpl. Alvin York.

Commissioned from the ranks in 1917, Woodfill had previously served in the Regular Army since enlisting in 1901. During the morning of October 13, 1918, finding himself and his company pinned down by sniper and machine gun fire from Cunel, Woodfill, a farm boy from Indiana who had grown up shooting squirrels off rail fences with his daddy's muzzle-loading rifle, squeezed off five shots from his rifle through the window of the church steeple, putting an end to that annoyance. Crawling from shell hole to shell hole, he next emptied another clip through a small hole knocked into the side of an abandoned stable, silencing that gun. He then stalked another machine gun firing from Cunel, diving into a shell hole contaminated with mustard gas along the way, finally shooting all six members of the crew from about 40 feet, the last with his .45 automatic. Woodfill next dispatched an *Oberleutnant* who was playing dead with his Colt .45 revolver (he was carrying two handguns at the time, his longtime favorite being the revolver). Stuffing the Heinie's Luger 9mm automatic in a pocket, he set out after another nest, dispatching its crew as he had the first. Next, Woodfill disarmed three young *Soldaten* bringing ammo forward, before sniping the five-man crew of a third machine gun. All the while, the scattered men of his company had been moving forward in support.

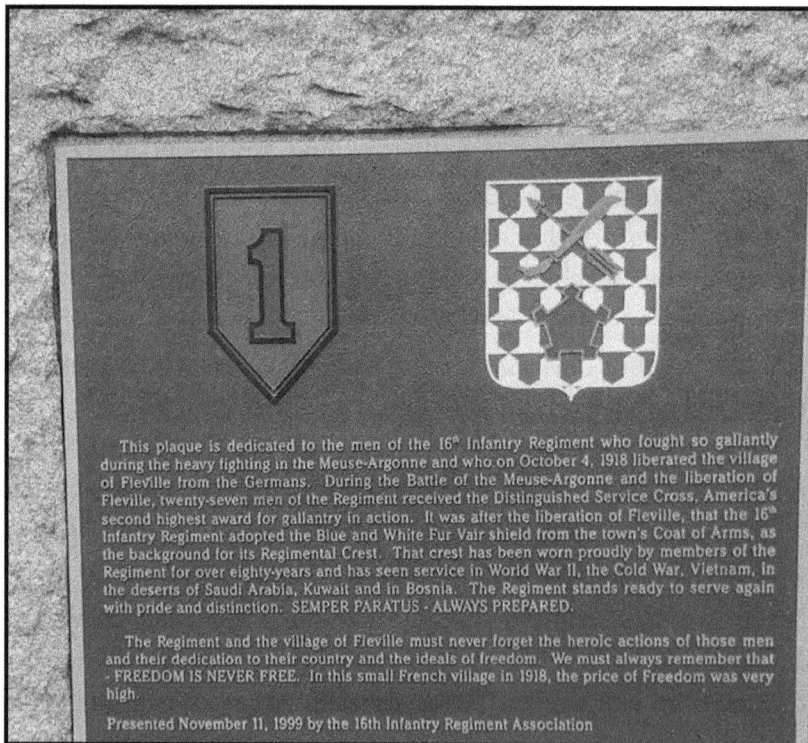

This plaque is dedicated to the men of the 16th Infantry Regiment who fought so gallantly during the heavy fighting in the Meuse-Argonne and who on October 4, 1918 liberated the village of Fleville from the Germans. During the Battle of the Meuse-Argonne and the liberation of Fleville, twenty-seven men of the Regiment received the Distinguished Service Cross, America's second highest award for gallantry in action. It was after the liberation of Fleville, that the 16th Infantry Regiment adopted the Blue and White Fur Vair shield from the town's Coat of Arms, as the background for its Regimental Crest. That crest has been worn proudly by members of the Regiment for over eighty-years and has seen service in World War II, the Cold War, Vietnam, in the deserts of Saudi Arabia, Kuwait and in Bosnia. The Regiment stands ready to serve again with pride and distinction. SEMPER PARATUS - ALWAYS PREPARED.

The Regiment and the village of Fleville must never forget the heroic actions of those men and their dedication to their country and the ideals of freedom. We must always remember that - FREEDOM IS NEVER FREE. In this small French village in 1918, the price of Freedom was very high.

Presented November 11, 1999 by the 16th Infantry Regiment Association

Small memorials are scattered throughout the Argonne Forest. This 1st Infantry Division monument commemorates the taking of Fléville, France. The 16th Infantry Regiment earned 27 Distinguished Service Crosses during the Meuse-Argonne campaign.

Lt. Samuel Woodfill. (Photo: Wikimedia)

As a finale, after his .45 auto jammed, he killed two Heinie gunners with their own pick-mattock entrenching tool. He next moved into the shattered woods northeast of Cunel before realizing that his decimated company was unsupported, leading him to withdraw back along his trail of destruction. He had waged his very personal vendetta while suffering from gas inhalation for which he was later hospitalized. Afterward Woodfill remembered having his gas mask strapped to his chest, but was reluctant to put it on because, if he did, he wouldn't be able to "see well enough to shoot."

One of the war's most decorated doughboys, Woodfill was awarded the Medal of Honor for his exploits and honored again by being chosen as a pallbearer at the dedication of the Tomb of the Unknowns.　After the war, he gave up his temporary commission so that he could finish his 30 years of service as a sergeant, thus earning an Army retirement and a secure life on his Indiana farm.

The victory came none too soon for "Black Jack" Pershing whose continued command of the AEF was coming under sharp criticism from both Clemenceau and Lloyd George.　Haig (and possibly Foch) wanted him replaced; however, as long as Secretary Baker, who was in France at this critical time representing President Wilson, had his back, there was nothing his enemies could do other than pray for his success.　About this time he seems to have despaired of victory as well.　One day while being driven in his staff car, "Black Jack" was heard to cry out to his dead wife, "Frankie, Frankie, my god, sometimes I don't know how I can go on."　But, go on he did.

Although the Meuse-Argonne campaign had become a meat grinder, the First Army had continued to grow to 592,300 combat troops despite an horrific number of casualties and an increasing number of stragglers, possibly as many as 100,000 at any one time.　The situation was serious enough that Pershing quietly issued an order calling for the shooting of any straggler if he ran in the face of the enemy.

By mid-October, the AEF totaled 1,256,478 men, prompting Pershing to create a Second Army, the command of which he gave to the hard-driving Robert Bullard.　"Black Jack" then removed himself as commander of the First Army, turning it over to Hunter Liggett, and became in effect an Army Group commander, on an equal footing with Gens. Haig and Pétain. Gens. Charles P. Summerall, James T. Dickman and John L.

Hines moved up to command corps, with changes cascading down the chain of command in their former divisions.

Liggett delayed what would be the First Army's final offensive until November 1 to give him an opportunity to assess his new command and to accommodate Gen. Gouraud's French Fourth Army.

When the offensive kicked off, the artillery preparation was impressive, even employing 14-inch naval guns mounted on railroad cars that tossed 1,400 pound shells into German rear areas for days before the attack, then using smaller guns to drop over 41 tons of gas shells on German artillery positions in the Bois de Bourgogne, effectively neutralizing them. The hard-driving Summerall, the former 1st ID artilleryman, now V Corps Commande, deployed over 600 artillery pieces to clear the way for his divisions.

The First Army attack on November 1 was in many ways a repeat of September 25 – a dawn attack covered by artillery barrages – excepting the number of front line divisions was reduced to seven, probably in response to the confusion and supply problems the earlier nine-division front had caused, and the first day's objectives were more modest. American tactics were now greatly refined. Two divisions, the 2nd and 89th, successfully altered their jump-off positions to frustrate German artillery countermeasures. Gen. Lejeune successfully employed night marches to disrupt German defenses in the Bois de Belval, a tactic not considered possible a month before.

The much maligned 79th ID was now re-inserted into the battle east of the Meuse River and given the daunting task of driving the Boche from Hill 378 ("Corn Willie" or "Corned Willie" Hill) that they had been using for artillery spotting. Yanks from 313th and 315th Infantries took the hill on November 7 and were still pushing east when the Armistice went into effect.

While the Second Army held a quiet section of the front between Port-sur-Seille and Fresnes awaiting orders to open the postponed attack toward Metz, the First Army gained most of its first day's objectives, then continued its advance in a wide sweeping arc to the northeast, its right flank anchored on the Meuse. German forces pulled back so rapidly, *Soldaten* deserting in ever larger numbers, their abandoned and destroyed equipment strewn along the roads, that it was difficult for the advancing Americans to maintain contact. By now, probably even the average doughboy suspected what their commanders already knew – the German war effort had collapsed and the Kaiser's new government was extending peace feelers to the Allies.

As far back as July, as the last of his spring offensives had foundered on the Marne, Ludendorff had despaired of victory. The tide of manpower had turned irreversibly against the German Empire; it could no longer replace its losses while the flood of arriving Yanks swelled the forces available to the Allies. Turning to the 70-year-old Paul von Hindenburg, titular head of the German Army, Ludendorff asked what they should do now, to which Hindenburg supposedly replied with biting sarcasm: "Do? Do! Make peace, you idiot!" Shortly after the Meuse-Argonne offensive kicked off in late September, both agreed that Germany should sue for peace, although at times Ludendorff balked.

Negotiations with President Wilson began in mid-October on the basis of his Fourteen Points. The president made it clear that he would not negotiate with the German Empire; the Kaiser would have to go. After intense internal struggles within the Imperial government between the peace factions represented by the newly appointed Chancellor, Prince Max of Baden and pro-war factions in the Army and Navy, mutinies aboard ships in the High Seas Fleet and Red revolutions in many German cities settled the issue in favor of the Chancellor. Wilhelm II, holed up in the Château de la Fraineuse in Spa, reluctantly abdicated on November 9, leaving for exile in Holland the next day. At the same time, a German armistice commission headed by Matthias Erzberger, a leader of the Catholic Centrist Party, met with French and British (no Americans were present) military leaders outside Compiègne and agreed to terms. Before dawn on November 11, the Germans filed into the railcar that Marshal Foch used as his command center to sign the armistice documents. The Allied terms were harsh amounting to a virtual unconditional surrender by the Reich. A ceasefire was finally to quiet the Western Front at 11:00, the eleventh hour of the eleventh day of the eleventh month.

Meanwhile, the drive toward Mézières/Sedan continued, leading to one last controversy in Liggett's First Army. Everyone wanted the honor of liberating Sedan – the French to avenge the debacle of 1870, Pershing to validate the AEF, and finally, Gens. Summerall and Parker to shed the glory on their commands, the V Corps and 1st ID. Whatever the motives, on November 5 Pershing had his G-3, Gen. Fox Conner, hand-deliver a directive to First Army HQ at Souilly stating that "General Pershing desires that the honor of entering Sedan should fall to the 1st American Army.... Boundaries will not be considered binding." Since Sedan was clearly in the I Corps' zone of operations, its commander, Gen. Joseph T. Dickman, assumed that his 42nd ID (now commanded by Brig. Gen. Douglas MacArthur who, because of his unconventional uniform, was mistaken for a German officer and temporarily arrested by a Lt. Black from the 1st ID) would have that honor. However, Gens. Summerall and Parker took the directive to mean that the race was on, winner take all, so Parker ordered his Big Red One to move on the city, crossing Corps' boundaries. The results were that on November 8 the two divisions found themselves at cross-purposes on Hill 252, a mile or so south of Sedan – Gen. Gouraud outraged and Summerall and Parker in hot water at Liggett's HQ. However, since the war ended three days later, no one, especially Pershing, now recovered from a bout with the flu, was inclined to press for an investigation.

What next? The Boche had signed an armistice, not an unconditional surrender as Pershing would have preferred (and was criticized for having suggested). An American military presence would be required in Europe until definitive treaties were agreed to and signed. That would take time, as would the disposal of American military supplies and the shutting down of the manpower pipeline. Meanwhile, on November 12, Pershing wrote out General Orders No. 203, addressed to the AEF, which began: "The enemy has capitulated. It is fitting that I address myself in thanks directly to the officers and soldiers of the American Expeditionary Forces who by their heroic efforts have made possible this glorious result." And heroic they were, for the casualties suffered by the AEF in the Meuse-Argonne campaign were shocking – in the U.S. First and Second Armies, during 47 days of combat, they numbered 122,063, a final figure not released by the War Department until 1926. Just less than half the AEF's combat deaths came in this one campaign, about half of what the American military suffered in seven years of war in Vietnam.

His war won, "Black Jack" to let off steam and savor the moment, hopped into his staff car and did what a million or so doughboys would loved to have done – he motored to Paris where, after fighting his way through crowds of Paris revelers with a group of friends, Charles Dawes, Jim Harbord, aide Carl Boyd and wife in tow, he attended a performance of "Zig Zag" at the Folies Bergère. Who knows, he possibly spent time with his mistress and later wife-to-be, the young Romanian portrait artist, Micheline Resco. In the days afterward, he made the rounds of Allied headquarters bestowing the Distinguished Service Medal on Foch, Haig and Pétain, all differences now forgiven, if not forgotten. He even embraced Clemenceau.

For the doughboys who only wanted to go home, life returned to a maddening, quasi-peacetime routine with training exercises and close-order drill. Eventually, Pershing relented, encouraging sporting contests, allowing the AEF to establish schools for the rank and file and officers alike to improve their education, and even allowing those qualified to enroll in European universities.

The Meuse-Argonne ABMC Cemetery is the largest in Europe.

A Third U.S. Army, some 240,000 Yanks strong, was quickly organized under the command of Gen. Joseph Dickman and then settled into Coblenz by the end of the first week of December where they would remain for five years as our "Watch on the Rhine."

"Black Jack" returned to the United States in early September 1919 to a hero's welcome. While he was still at sea, Congress voted to confer the rank of General of the Armies, the highest honor it could bestow on America's returning hero; only one other was previously bestowed – George Washington. Only four months after honoring Alvin York with a ticker tape parade, New York City accorded Pershing and the AEF an equally enthusiastic welcome home. On September 10, led by Pershing on horseback, the Big Red One, long his favorite division (with a provisional regiment made up of representatives from the other combat divisions), marched down 5th Avenue between throngs of cheering Americans and into memory. It was reminiscent of the parade of the victorious Army of the Potomac down Washington's Pennsylvania Avenue some half century earlier. (Note: Pershing rehearsed his role by riding at the head of a similar victory parade in Paris before sailing home.) Other AEF units held their own victory parades when they reached their home states.

Although it was 1923 before the last American troops left Germany, by the 4th of July 1919, 2,700,000 doughboys had been discharged, leaving for home with a uniform, a coat, a pair of shoes and a $60 discharge bonus. Those men who had served overseas could also keep their tin hats and gas masks as souvenirs. Sadly, black doughboys, fewer than a dozen, came home to face lynch mobs for being too "uppity" in their Army uniforms, behavior seen as a challenge to the Southern white social order.

America had not quite heard the last from the AEF. A decade after their home coming, many veterans, now calling themselves the BEF (Bonus Expeditionary Force), unemployed because of the Great Depression, demonstrated in Washington in 1932 for early payment of another bonus they had been promised for their service. Congress was unsympathetic (a bill to move up the date of the payment was defeated in the Senate) and President Herbert Hoover ordered the BEF's temporary encampment on the banks of the Anacostia River removed. Then Army Chief-of-Staff Gen. Douglas MacArthur and Maj. George S. Patton were the Regular Army officers who commanded the troops that carried out the order. However, four years later Congress ordered the bonus paid, overriding the veto of President Franklin D. Roosevelt to accomplish that end.

Meuse-Argonne Battlefield: Museums, Cemetery and Memorials

Le Mémorial de Verdun

State of Missouri Memorial, Varennes-en-Argonne

The Museum of Mine Warfare, Varennes-en-Argonne

Meuse-Argonne American Cemetery, Varennes-en-Argonne

Montfaucon American Monument, Montfaucon

Sommepy American Monument

2nd ID boulder-markers (2) near Sommepy-Tahure and Blanc Mont ridge

2nd ID boulder-markers (2) between Mouzon and Moulins-Saint-Hubert

2nd ID boulder-marker off of D4 between Sommerance and Landres-et-Saint Georges

German military cemetery at Saint-Étienne-á-Arnes, north of Blanc Mont ridge

State of Pennsylvania Memorial, Nantillois

4th ID stele, Nantillois

5th ID stele, Doulcon

315th IR (79th ID) Memorial plaque, Nantillois

317th IR (79th ID) stele, Nantillois

316th Infantry (79th ID) monument, Sivry-sur-Meuse

Signs at "The Lost Battalion" site, Argonne Forest

Sign and plaque at Sgt. Alvin York site, Châtel-Chéhéry

Pvt. Henry Gunther memorial stele, Chaumont-devant-Damvillers

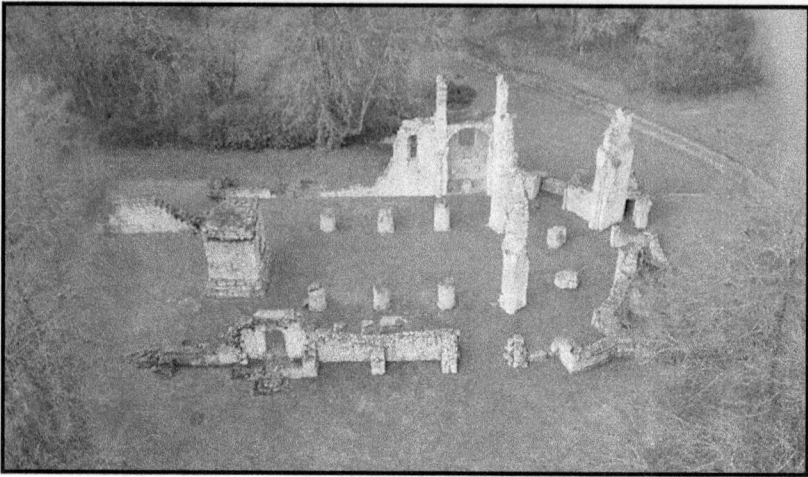

Destroyed cathedral view from the top of Montfaucon American Monument.

THE ARMISTICE AND THE PEACE

The famous Armistice of the 11th hour (Paris time, of course) of the 11th day of the 11th month marked the end of the shooting war, but not military operations. It certainly was not literally peace since economic warfare in the form of a naval blockade of Germany continued for many months. Tens of thousands of doughboys spent their 1918 Christmases occupying the Rhineland alongside troops from the other Allied nations. Set to expire on Dec. 13, the armistice agreement had to be renewed three times before the formal signing of the Treaty of Versailles on Jan. 10, 1920 finally voided it. However, a state of suspended belligerency formally existed between the Entente and the other Central Powers until the Treaties of Saint-Germain-en-Laye (Austria, July 16, 1920), Neuilly (Bulgaria, Aug. 9, 1920), Trianon (Hungary, July 26, 1921) and Lausanne (Turkey, Aug. 6, 1924) finally went into effect, even though all had been signed a year or more earlier.

The United States formally ended its belligerency when President Warren G. Harding signed a joint resolution of Congress to that effect on July 2, 1921. The U.S. Senate's earlier failure to ratify the Treaty of Versailles that had ended the Entente's war with the German Empire made that resolution necessary.

But all the complicated peacemaking was in the future when it became apparent to the German High Command in October that the war was lost and that the preservation of the Army as a countervailing force to the growing chaos inside Germany was now all that really mattered. On October 4, the Kaiser's cousin, Prince Max von Baden, who had taken office as Chancellor the day before, made contact with the State Department in an effort to feel out Wilson on the possibility of a peace agreement based on Wilson's Fourteen Points, but time had run out for the German Empire. Sailors in the High Seas Fleet at Wilhelmshaven and Kiel mutinied at the end of October and spread the discontent south where peace demonstration broke out in the streets of many cities. Already the Austrians and Bulgarians had requested an armistice.

Nor were the British and the French about to let the peace-making slip from their hands into those of some "Johnny-come-lately" American idealist, parts of whose Fourteen Point peace plan they quietly and bitterly opposed. Events now moved rapidly, but maybe not rapidly enough for the 6,600 doughboys who were killed during the armistice negotiations, fighting an enemy that was about to concede defeat, as the Kaiser forced Ludendorff into retirement in late October opening the way for peace negotiations to begin in earnest.

To clear the way for negotiations, the German politicians now in power sent the unwilling Kaiser into exile in Holland, where he spent the remainder of his life.

At the urging of the military, Prince Max appointed a commission of four to travel to France to negotiate terms the Allies would accept to end the fighting. Headed by Matthias Erzberger, recently appointed to hear the propaganda ministry, the commission of six, traveling slowly in five automobiles that continually broke down, reached and crossed the French lines during the night of November 7. The Germans envoys were quickly transferred to a train that proceeded to a forested area outside Compiègne, forty miles north of Paris, where it was parked on a siding. Shortly thereafter, Foch's private train pulled into a nearby parallel siding. Duckboards were laid over the muddy ground between the two so negotiations could begin.

Over the next three days, interrupted only by the difficulties the Germans had in communicating with Berlin and the periodic movement of the trains to replenish water supplies (each train consisted of three cars — a saloon car for meals, a parlor car and a wagon-lit for sleeping), Foch, aided by his Chief-of-Staff, Gen. Maxime Weygand and backed by Premier Georges Clemenceau in Paris, laid out the Allied terms. The terms: the surrender of various weapons, aircraft and capital ships of the *Kaiserliche Marine;* the surrender of all occupied territories including Alsace and Lorraine; a continuation of the Allied naval blockade and the occupation of the Rhineland being the principal demands in the 34 articles. The only changes the French would allow were minor points such as the exact number of aircraft and other weapons that were to be surrendered. Berlin instructed the Erzberger to strive for the best terms he could, but to sign no matter what. All parties present (French, British and German since no other nations on either side were represented) signed the Armistice papers at about 05:10 in the morning of November 11 at a table in the parlor car Foch was using for his mobile HQ; the fighting was to cease at 11:00.

The actual Armistice was in some ways anti-climatic since the United Press International news service had broadcast false information on the 8th that an armistice had been concluded. Celebrations had broken out around the world as the news quickly spread. The revelers, unfortunately, woke up the next morning with hangovers only to learn that the fighting continued. (One American was shot and killed after a bar argument over the truth of the rumor.)

Head of UPI in France, Roy W. Howard, had gotten wind of a news release by the semi-official German news agency, Wolff Telegraphic Bureau, that the Armistice Commission had left for France. He was in Brest waiting to sail for the United States, away from his Paris office and French and American censors. Rumors were flying everywhere that the Armistice had been concluded, so Howard, not wanting to be scooped, sent off a cable to the UPI office in New York, bypassing the usual censors, to that effect.   Rewritten in New York for UPI distribution, the bulletin read:

"Paris, November 7. — The Allies and Germany signed an armistice at 11 o'clock this morning.   Hostilities ceased at 2 o'clock this afternoon."

The Americans took Sedan before the armistice became effective.

Of course, none of it was true, but once the UPI had put it on the wire, the worldwide celebration began. By the time Howard realized his error, it was too late to stop the premature celebrations.

But, what about the doughboys on the front lines? Pershing and his staff (and undoubtedly the German High Command as well) thought that if the war continued for a few more days they could force the Germans into an unconditional surrender, so they punted by instructing the field commanders to keep up the pressure, but giving no timetable for stopping the offensive. There were 16 American divisions fighting the Krauts on the morning of November 11. Seven of the division commanders ordered operations to cease when they learned of the impending armistice; nine chose to continue the war to 11:00, decisions that resulted in hundreds of needless deaths and casualties. (In defense of the nine commanders, no one knew for sure that the Armistice would hold or that it was anything more than a German ploy to gain time for a withdrawal behind their border.) As a final salute to the Boche, the crews of the 14″ American railway guns fired off a last salvo seconds before the armistice went into effect.

Marines from the V Corps were ordered to sneak across the Meuse during the night of November 10 -11 in a rather pointless attack; Gen. Summerall, their commander, was never reluctant to push his men to the limit. Two battalions of the 5th Marines managed to cross the river between Mouzon and Autreville in the darkness, but Kraut artillery destroyed their footbridges leaving the 67th Company stranded. Under intense shell fire, the surviving leathernecks held out until the Armistice ended the fighting later that morning.

Gen. Robert Bullard, 2nd Army Commander, who ordered four of his divisions (7th, 28th, 33rd and 92nd) to push their attacks across the Meuse right up to 11:00, recounted in his memoirs that on the morning of November 11 he and an aide traveled to the front to witness the last shots, "to hear the crack of the last guns in the greatest war of all ages . . . I stayed until 11:00 a.m., when, all being over, I returned to my headquarters, thoughtful and feeling lost."

Officially, the last combat death of a doughboy in the Great War was Pvt. Henry Gunther, a German/American assigned to Company A· 313th Infantry, 79th ID. Recently demoted and distrusted by his comrades, he may have been trying to redeem himself when he charged a Boche machine gun nest alone, firing his BAR, only minutes before 11:00. The German gunners tried to warn him off, and then, ended his suicide charge with a short burst from their Maxim. For a more complete account of the travails of Pvt. Gunther see William Walker's, "Betrayal at Little Gibraltar" (2016).

When the soldiers on both sides got word on the Armistice, feelings ran the gamut from elation to disbelief. Although sternly prohibited, fraternization took place all along the Western Front. Doughboys were always willing to trade cigarettes and food for souvenirs. Of course, some units failed to get notice of the impending Armistice, so they continued fighting into the afternoon. The "War to End all Wars" continued in central Africa for weeks after the signing in Compiègne.

Sites connected to the Armistice and the Treaty:

Clairière de l'Armistice: Compiègne
Château de Versailles: The Hall of Mirrors
2nd Division boulders (2) south of Mouzon
Fifth Corps stone marker south of Mouzon
　　Pvt. Henry Gunther memorial stele

The Services of Supply

It's easy to overlook the essential contributions of the SOS to the successes of the AEF, but it's obvious that the logistical tail of an army that was projected to reach 2,000,000 men in 1919 had to be enormous, varied and efficient. The AEF used three ports for the most of their supply effort on the Bay of Biscay: St. Nazaire, La Pallice (Rochefort) and Pauillac (Bordeaux). These ports had the advantages of being far enough south to be out of normal U-boat range, having rail connections to the interior and leaving the Channel ports to the British. SOS immediately began to improve the AEF's ability to supply its combat troops by improving the capacities of those ports, building warehouses at the ports and depots along the rail lines, improving those lines by laying new track, repairing French rolling stock and importing thousands of American locomotives and railcars for assembly in France. At Gièvres, east of Tours, SOS maintained a facility that deloused and repaired worn doughboy uniforms. That unit was part of an enormous complex that employed some 20,000 personnel who worked in the 165 warehouses. SOS also strung hundreds of miles of telephone lines, maintained the switchboards and even employed dozens of bilingual American women to operate them.

Gen. Pershing commanded the SOS along with all his other duties, but the job threatened to overwhelm him. In July 1918, Secretary Baker made the pointed suggestion that he relinquish that authority in favor of Gen. George W. Goethals, famous as builder of the Panama Canal. Extremely reluctant to give up control of his seriously failing supply organization, Pershing responded by relieving the SOS commander, Maj. Gen. Francis Kernan, and replacing him with an old friend, his former chief-of-staff, Maj. Gen. James Harbord. Harbord, who had just come close to wrecking the 2nd ID during the Soissons battle, took the new job and, by all accounts, performed admirably in his new position for the rest of the war, although the SOS never performed as well as GHQ hoped.

Two other patriotic Americans were also important to the success of the SOS – Charles G. Dawes and William W. Atterbury. Dawes, who had known Pershing since his days as head of the University of Nebraska's officer training program, now a wealthy lawyer and banker, accepted a Major's commission in the 17th Engineers (he ended the war as a Brigadier General) to sail to France as a member of the SOS. He headed the General Purchasing Board for the AEF, the organization that oversaw the procurement of supplies of all kinds from overseas sources. Immediately after the Armistice, Dawes became a member of the Liquidation Commission that oversaw the sale of much of that surplus property in France. When queried about his procurements activities by a Congressional committee in 1921, he famously blurted out "Hell and Maria, we weren't keeping a set of books over there, we were trying to win a war." Atterbury, the vice-president in charge of operations for the Pennsylvania Railroad since 1911, had gotten to know Pershing while helping with transportation problems during the Mexican Punitive Expedition. Now commissioned as a Brigadier General, he built and operated the SOS's extensive rail network in France.

Both highly decorated men resigned their commissions in 1919 to return to civilian life – Dawes later to author the "Dawes Plan" revising German post-war reparations for which he shared the 1925 Nobel Peace Prize and then to serve as Vice-President of the United States. Atterbury eventually became president of the Pennsylvania Railroad and, as such, graced the cover of "Time" in 1933.

Atterbury's railroad career is remembered with a bronze plaque in Philadelphia's 30th Street Station, formerly part of the Pennsylvania Railroad system.

THE BATTLEFIELD TOURS

We decided that in the interest of efficiency to create two tours for visiting the various AEF battlefield cemeteries and memorials in France and Belgium. The Northern Tour will take you north from Paris, ending in Belgium. The Eastern tour will take two days to complete if you decide to visit all the sites relating to the Meuse-Argonne campaign. A limitation of this approach is that descriptions of those sites do not immediately follow our summaries of the battles, but we feel that the separate section for tours is a more useful way of organizing the book. We have also listed the major memorials and cemeteries at the end of those chapters dealing with individual battles.

Of course, each tour does not have to be followed in its entirety to benefit from the experience. It's very possible to take day trips from any of the cities you choose as a base to visit as many nearby sites as your time and interest dictate. Some sites in and near Paris can be visited in a day. Those further afield are more easily reached if you base yourself in a nearby city, e.g., Brussels, Ghent, Château-Thierry, Reims or Verdun. Doing so will save you hours of driving time and allow you to explore the sites at your leisure. Nevertheless, we have laid out the tours along two routes radiating out from Paris, the most likely arrival-destination city in France. We hope this organization helps you plan your visit to these sites more easily and efficiently.

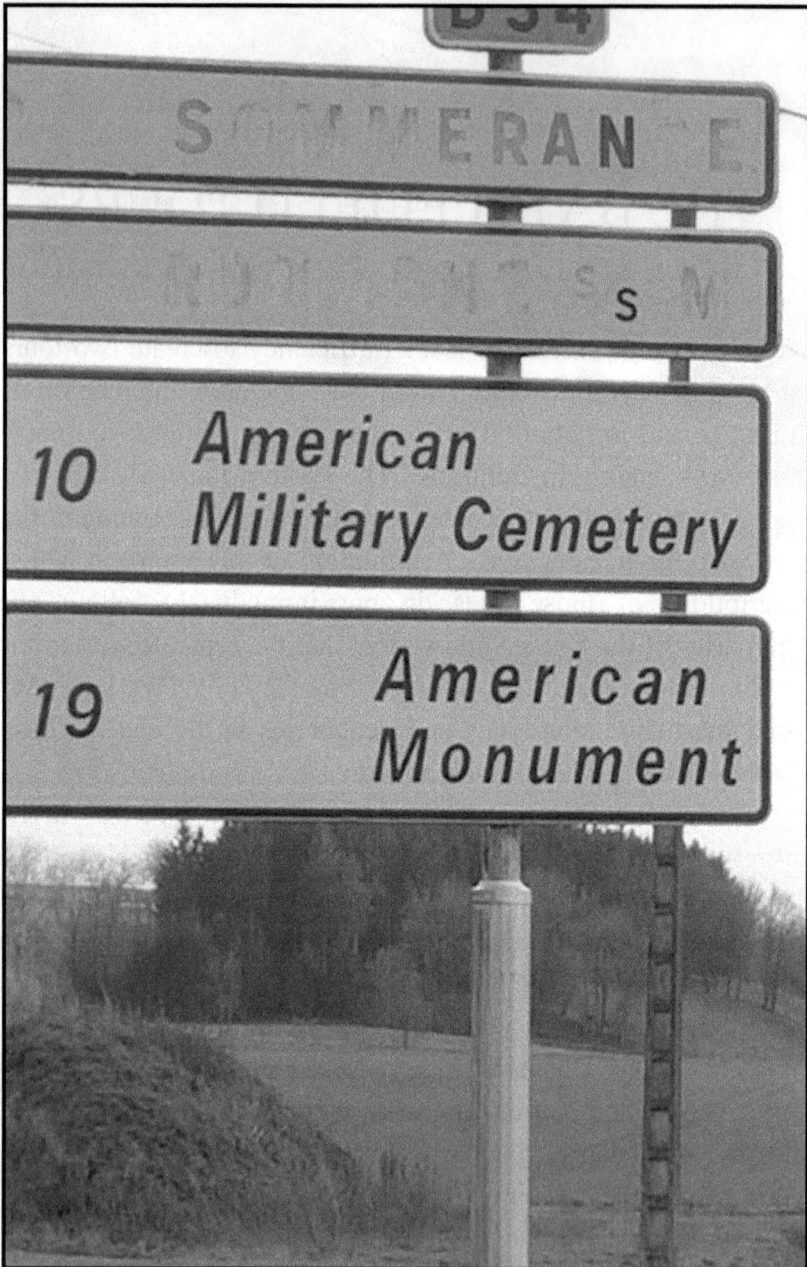

Watch for direction signs carefully in rural areas—if you miss one—the next opportunity to turn around may not be very several kilometers.

The Northern Tour:

The sites of interest along this route are best accessed by driving north from Paris on the Autoroute du Nord A1-E15.

Compiègne: Clairière de l'Armistice

A contemporary duplicate of the carriage in which Foch and Erzberger signed the Armistice resides today in an enclosed pavilion just outside Compiègne. Nearby, a horizontal slab resting between rails marks the spot where the rail car sat on the morning of November 11, 1918. The history of this exhibit is curious to say the least.

The French government put the *wagon-salon* on display shortly after the war, first at the Invalides in Paris, and later near Compiègne where it sat in an enclosed building, and there it rested in relative obscurity until 1940 when Adolf Hitler motored to Compiègne at the end of June to accept the surrender of France. Hitler sought to humiliate the French nation by forcing its representatives to sign the articles of surrender inside the very *wagon-salon* where the German commissioners had abjectly signed the Armistice 22 years before.

The Führer was still at his advanced headquarters in Belgium (FHQu *Wolfsschlucht*) when he learned that the French had requested an armistice. In triumph, he raised his right leg and stamped it on the ground. A cameraman, Walter Frentz, caught the moment on film and later released it to the world, but the real coup came when a Canadian film technician, John Grierson, altered the propaganda clip to make it look as if the Führer was dancing in triumph over the French defeat. And, to complete the Allied propaganda effort, the whole incident was portrayed as taking place in Compiègne where the 1940 armistice agreement was eventually signed. Hitler made a formal appearance at

Compiègne, but was already off on whirlwind tours to Paris and various WWI sites where he had fought before the actual signing. (By Googling "Hitler at Compiègne" you can turn up a number of highly edited YouTube film clips of the 1940 surrender.)

Nevertheless, Hitler's visit to Compiègne and the 1940 Armistice signed there brought the *wagon-salon* back to the attention of the world, so the Nazis removed it to a Berlin park where the party faithful could relive the memorable events of 1918 and 1940. Unfortunately for historical preservationists, the car was destroyed during an Allied bombing raid in 1943.

The Clairière de l'Armistice site was itself leveled by the Nazis, except for the Alsace-Lorraine monument, which was carted off to Berlin in pieces.

In 1949, French museum officials reconstituted the Armistice site, putting a *wagon-salon* on display that was represented as the original. Only when a member (most likely Rose Coombs, a long time IWM employee and a WWI historian) of a group from Britain's Imperial War Museum crawled under the coach to check its serial number and determined that it was not the original, but an identical, WWI-era *wagon-salon* that had been tricked out as Foch's had been in 1918.

Despite the subterfuge surrounding the duplicate rail coach, or maybe because of it, a visit to the Clairière de l'Armistice is certainly worthwhile. Besides the *wagon-salon* itself, there is the granite slab commemorating the Allied victory in 1918 and another slab, resting between two rails, marking the site where the coach stood on November 11, 1918 and June 22, 1940. The site is also home to a small Armistice museum, a well-preserved Renault FT17 tank and a statue of Maréchal Foch.

The attractions are open daily, except Tuesdays, from 10:00 a.m. to 6:00 p.m. from April to mid-September. Everything closes 30 minutes earlier the remainder of the year. For current information go to the website: musee-armistice-14-18.fr.

Compiègne is most easily reached from Paris by taking the autoroute A1 north to exit 10 (66 km). Follow your GPS or Google Earth directions to wend your way east across the city to the Clairière de l'Armistice site.

Cantigny American Monument

This ABMC memorial consists of a truncated white stone block located in a small park in the village of Cantigny. GPS coordinates: N49 39.803 E2 29.472.

Also in the village there is a memorial to the 28th Infantry, a granite pedestal surmounted by an American infantryman, rifle with fixed bayonet in hand. One face of the pedestal bears the dedication inscription, a second with a rampant Lion (the insignia of the 28th Infantry) and on a third, the name "Cantigny." The monument was dedicated on July 5, 2007 and sponsored by the 28th Regiment Association, the McCormick Tribune Foundation, the Cantigny First Division Foundation and the Village of Cantigny, obviously the organizations responsible for its creation.

An older roadside memorial dedicated to the 1st ID stands just east of Cantigny on D26. It consists of a shaft surmounted by an eagle with draped wings standing on what appears to be an upright artillery shell. This memorial is one of five erected by the 1st Division Association in the post-war years, the other four being located on different Big Red One battlefields.

Look for the 1st ID Memorial on your right, three to four kilometers outside of Montdidier.

Australian Corps Memorial, Le Hamel

The Australian Corps Memorial, with the flags of Australia, Great Britain, France, Canada and the United States flying overhead, stands just east of the village of Le Hamel, a short drive east of Amiens.

If you are coming from Calais take the A16 south around Amiens where you can pick up the A29 east. Exit the autoroute at Villers-Bretonneux and drive north on D23 toward Fouilloy. Just south of Fouilloy, turn east on D71, which will take you to Le Hamel. The Memorial is just east of the village off the Chemin de Sailly Laurette.

From Paris, take the A16 north to Amiens.

Somme American Cemetery, Bony

Some 1,844 of the dead from American units attached to the British Army in Picardy and many doughboys killed in the 1st ID operations against the town of Cantigny, are buried in this 14.3-acre cemetery. The cemetery is divided into four sections around a central flagpole, divided by walks. The small chapel (a low, blockish tower) is entered through large, bronze doors decorated with eagles. Inside the names of 333 missing are inscribed on the walls.

The Somme American Cemetery is located in Picardy just southwest of the village of Bony and about 2.5 km west of highway D1044, between the cities of St. Quentin and Cambrai.

Maybe the simplest way to visit this cemetery and the nearby Bellicourt American Memorial by auto is to take the A1-E15-E19 (Autoroute du Nord) north from Paris. Exit the A1 between Amiens and St. Quentin (exit 13) and drive east to St. Quentin where you can pick up D1044 (N4) north toward Bellicourt and Cambrai. (Bellicourt is the site of both a British monument [in town] and a cemetery just to the west.) A kilometer north of Bellicourt you will pass the turnoff to the Bellicourt Monument. In a little less than 2 km farther north, turn west on D442 to Bony. The Somme American Cemetery is just west of the village. GPS coordinates: N49 59.103 E3 12.798.

Bellicourt American Monument, Bellicourt

This low, severe, rectangular, marble monument, decorated with neoclassical sculptures, commemorates the 90,000 American soldiers who served with British forces in WWI. It stands over a canal tunnel built in the time of Napoleon I. A map of American operations is engraved on one side, while the names of individual battles are inscribed around the base. An orientation table is located to one side.

The early 19th Century tunnel passing under both Bellicourt and Bony anchored this section of the Hindenburg Line, a defensive position German armies fell back on after the collapse of the Spring 1918 Offensive (in Picardy, known as Operation Michael). The U.S. 27th and 30th IDs attacked here on September 29 and, with the aid of the Australians, broke the German defenses.

Driving directions are the same as those for the Somme American cemetery, a couple of kilometers to the northwest. GPS coordinates: N49 58.511 E3 13.919.

Soissons Battlefield

There is very little today to mark the passage of the doughboys south of Soissons. Veterans of the 2nd ID placed one of its boulder markers just north of Vierzy (off D72), where their advance ground to a halt on the 18th. The bronze star is missing from the boulder. There is no American cemetery nearby, but the British sited one just west of Buzancy. The battlefield is most easily reached today by driving north on the D1 from Château-Thierry.

Oudenaarde (Audenarde) American Monument

This smallish, yellow-limestone monument is located in a small park in a commercial area in the Belgian city of Oudenaarde, which is located 60 km west of Brussels. The monument commemorates the 40,000 Americans from the 37th and 91st IDs along with the 53rd Field Artillery Brigade who were attached to the Belgian Army in October and November 1918. The monument bears the names of the AEF units above the shield of the United States and is flanked by two stylized eagles. Below is the dedication that reads:

ERECTED BY
THE UNITED STATES
OF AMERICA
TO COMMEMORATE
THE SERVICE OF
AMERICAN TROOPS
WHO FOUGHT IN
THIS VICINITY
OCT. 30 - NOV.11, 1918

Both Divisions fought their way from Waregem across the Scheldt River, with the 91st ID taking Oudenaarde on November 2-3, whereupon both divisions went into reserve. They moved forward again on the 10th, just before the Armistice.

The monument is located in the center of Oudenaarde off Generaal Pershingstraat; it's not easy to find. If you enter the town from Brussels on N8, drive cross the Lys River, and then exit N8 on N453. Turn east and then north on N453 until you reach the small park off Generaal Pershingstraat. GPS coordinates: N50 50.798 E3 36.142.

Flanders Field American Cemetery
This small, 6.2-acre cemetery, the only WWI American cemetery in Belgium, is located not far west of Oudenaarde, some 66 kilometers west of Brussels off autoroute A14 between Ghent and Lille. It contains 368 graves, mostly the dead from the U.S. 91st ID that fought near here. A memorial building enclosing a chapel stands in the Cemetery's center with rows of headstones

surrounding it. The names of 43 missing-in-action are inscribed on its interior walls surrounded by lovely mosaics.

American President Barack Obama visited this cemetery on March 26, 2014 with His Majesty King Philippe of Belgium and his Prime Minister, Elio Di Rupo. As he closed his remarks, the President recited the last lines of Canadian doctor Lt. Col. John McCrae's famous poem:

"To you from failing hands we throw
The torch; be yours to hold it high
If ye break faith with us who die
We shall not sleep, though poppies grow
In Flanders fields."

Then, the President read the reply written by an American woman, Moina Michael, "the poppy lady", who memorialized the red Flanders poppy as the symbol for The Great War:

"Oh! You who sleep in 'Flanders Fields,'
Sleep sweet — to rise anew!
We caught the torch you threw
And holding high, we keep the Faith
With All who died."

Contact the cemetery staff at Wortegemseweg 117, 8790, Waregem, Belgium. Phone: +32(0) 5 660 1122,

To reach the cemetery by automobile from Brussels, take the A 10-E 40 west out of the city toward Ghent. There, pick up the A14-E17 southwest to Waregem. From Oudenaarde we suggest that you to use the directions provided by Google Earth or your GPS device. The cemetery is on the southeast edge of Waregem. GPS coordinates: N50 52.424 E3 27.218.

The Eastern Tour: Day One

The first day of our Eastern Tour takes you east from Paris on the N3 or the A4-E50, Autoroute de L'Est, to Meaux, then to the A4 to exits 19 and 20 near Château-Thierry and then on to Verdun. In the following days, based out of Verdun, you can visit the Meuse-Argonne battlefield and other sites in the area. There is also frequent train service from Paris to Meaux, Château-Thierry and Verdun, but you will have to arrange for tours or a rental car from those cities to visit the memorials and cemeteries in the area.

Meaux

The American Monument

This stunning 74.5 foot high sculpture of a nude female figure stands in an open park that allows the visitor an unobstructed view. It is a depiction of Marianne, the symbol of the French nation, her head thrown back in anguish, holding a dead child in her lap.

The WWI Memorial in Atlantic City, N.J. is home to a 9-foot bronze replica.

Musée de la Grande Guerre du Pays de Meaux

This very good WWI museum opened recently and is located in the same park as the American Monument above.

Meaux is easily accessible from Paris by train; taking a cab to the museum and the American Monument is then your simplest option. The trip to Meaux from Paris Est takes about half an hour and the trains run all day.

If you decide to drive, take N3 out of Paris to the major roundabout on the outskirts of Meaux, which you leave on D1005 to the north. Follow your Google Earth or GPS directions to the park.

Château-Thierry

3rd U.S. Infantry Division Memorial, Avenue Jules Lefebvre
This rather stark memorial to the 3rd ID is the second to be erected in Château-Thierry, the first apparently badly damaged by French combat engineers when they blew the bridge over the Marne in June 1940. The new memorial consists of an upright stele flanked by stone walls. The stele carries the inscription IN MEMORIAM over a vertical sword and the dates 1917-1918 and 1942-1945. The flanking walls bear the inscription: "TO THE HEROIC DEEDS OF THE THIRD INFANTRY DIVISION UNITED STATES ARMY WORLD WAR I WORLD WAR II."

War damage remains on a cathedral south of Château-Thierry.

A half-scale wicker biplane installed in front of the memorial represents the Nieuport 28 that Lt. Quentin Roosevelt, eldest son of former President Theodore Roosevelt, flew when he crashed in the countryside near the town. The present memorial was erected in 1961 by The Society of the 3rd Infantry Division.

(A stele commemorating the famous leader of the French resistance, Jean Moulin, stands across Jules Lefebvre from the Memorial.)

To visit the Memorial if you enter the town via the Avenue de Soissons, take the west exit (Avenue Jules Lefebvre) from the roundabout closest to the Marne for a short distance to the Memorial, which is on your right. There is ample parking nearby.

The original 3rd ID memorial stood in the center of the roundabout just north of the bridge over the Marne where a statue of Château-Thierry's favorite son, the fabulist Jean de La Fontaine, now resides.

Maison de l'Amitié Franco Américaine, 2 place des États-Unis.

This odd little institution was the post-war brainchild of the Reverend Julian S. Wadsworth, a member of the Board of Foreign Missions of the Methodist Episcopal Church. It was one of a number of efforts by the Methodists in postwar France to render various kinds of aid to shattered French people. Château-Thierry was a natural spot for such an enterprise because of the fighting by American doughboys in and nearby the town. The MAFA, as it became known was an all-purpose institution patterned, one must assume, on the urban settlement houses that had been so popular in the United States at the turn of the century. Wadsworth had his board acquire the war-torn and abandoned Hôtel de l'Elephant, renovate and open it for business. (He initially found two dead Germans and, five months later, 46 sticks of dynamite in the wrecked building.)

The MAFA offered the services of a nurse, a daycare center, Boy Scout and Campfire Girls programs, a reading room and library, a small military museum, social clubs and cultural events. Its aim was to help the *Castelthéodoriciens* (as the residents of Château-Thierry style themselves) and promote Franco-American friendship.

The Methodists donated the operation to the town in 1930, but by 2000 the building had again fallen into disrepair so the city closed it. However, the people of Château-Thierry raised the funds for its second renovation and the new MAFA (now the Maison de l'Amitié France-Amérique (correcting Wadsworth's French!) opened again for business on November 10, 2015 with U.S. Ambassador Jane D. Hartley in attendance.

Today, it is a very different institution – the first floor is given over to the local tourist office and the second to a small museum devoted to the life and times of Lt. Quentin Roosevelt, who was killed when his Nieuport 28 crashed near Chamery, some 17 miles away. For almost a hundred years, the Maison had exhibited parts of Roosevelt's biplane in its small museum, however, recently doubt has been cast on the authenticity of the engine on display (a water-cooled Hispano-Suiza) because no Nieuport 28 was ever known to be flown in combat with that engine.

(Quentin's death is also commemorated with a fountain in Chamery, and also a memorial cross in the village of Sancy-les-Cheminots [20 kilometers northeast of Soissons, off the N2 highway] that was repaired after the war with financial help from the Roosevelt family.)

In 1955, Quentin's remains were reburied in the Normandy American Cemetery next to his younger brother, Brig. Gen. Theodore Roosevelt, Jr., who died of a heart attack in Normandy, a month after D-Day, 1944. Teddy, Jr., who served with the Big Red One in the Great War and then, as the 4th ID's Assistant Commander in 1944, was posthumously awarded the Medal of

Honor for his heroic actions on Utah Beach, where he landed with the first wave.

Honoring Wadsworth's original intentions, today's Maison provides space for local children to learn English. Phone: 03 23 83 51 14.

If you enter Château-Thierry from the north on the Avenue de Soissons, you can turn into the place de États-Unis (a large municipal parking lot) shortly before you reach the roundabout near the river bank. The Maison is at the far eastern end of the place. Check with the tourist office about the museum's opening and closing times.

Demarcation Stones

The idea of creating these small markers (known as *demarcatiepalen* in Belgium and *bornes du front* in France) originated with French sculptor Paul Moreau-Vauthier. His low, gnome-like, stone obelisks (some 240 originally planned) topped off with stone helmets, were to mark the lines of departure where the great Allied counter-offensive of September 1918 began. In all, 120 were set in place between 1921 and 1930 then, funds and interest in the project petered out. In a search conducted earlier in this century, battlefield sleuth Rik Scherpenberg located the 119 (some badly damaged) that are still in existence today, 96 in France and 23 in Belgium.

The first marker, set in place on November 11, 1921, now badly worn, stands in Château-Thierry beside the roundabout at the bottom of the Avenue de Soissons under a contemporary road sign pointing the way to Brasles. All the markers are similar, having carved canteens and gas mask cases on the sides with exploding grenades at the corners; only the helmets vary according to the nationality of the soldiers who had fought in nearby salients. They bear the inscription, *"Ici fut repoussé l'envahisseur"* — "From here the invader was driven back." These marker stones also stand at Vaux, Reims and St. Mihiel, among other locations. For more complete information on the Demarcation Stones go to the website: greatwar.co.uk.

Other famous French military road-markers include those that line the route from Bar-le-Duc to Verdun, the Voie Sacrée, and following the path of the U.S. Third Army (1944) from Normandy to Belgium, the Voie de la Liberté.

A stele on the same roundabout at the bottom of Avenue de Soissons featuring a haunting face in bas-relief with the words "SOUVIENS-TOI" ("REMEMBER"), commemorates French citizens deported to various Nazi death camps during the 1940s occupation.

Château-Thierry American Monument

This spectacular monument is an impressively large, colonnaded structure, designed by Paul Cret, that stands atop Hill 204 west of Château-Thierry presents the visitor with a lovely view of the town and the Marne valley from its terraces.

Its Château-Thierry American Monument has a commanding view of the city.

The east face bears bas-reliefs of a stylized eagle and the shield of the United States over the inscription "TIME SHALL

NOT DIM THE GLORY OF THEIR DEEDS" and an incised map of American military operations in the Aisne-Marne salient. A useful orientation table is inscribed on the east-facing terrace just below the monument.

The west face is dominated by two monumental female figures in classical garb, hands entwined, representing the nations of France and the United States.

Both Gens. Pershing and Harbord spoke briefly at its dedication in 1937. The ABMC website has a brief film of the dedication ceremony.

Renovations to the visitor contact station are presently underway (2016) and may impact your access to the terraces. The renovated contact station will encompass a 2,000 sq, ft, exhibition area devoted to interpreting American participation in WWI in Europe. It is expected to be fully open by the spring of 2017.

The Monument can be reached from either exit 19 or 20 off the A4, and then, follow signs to the entrance. GPS: W49 2.528 E3 22.250.

Belleau Wood — U.S. Marine Memorial

A modest memorial to the marines of the 4th Marine Brigade, 2nd ID, specifically those leathernecks from 5th and 6th Marine Regiments, who fought here in June 1918, stands in the middle of the road that traverses Belleau Wood. The marines attacked German positions in the Wood until the Boche withdrew on June 26; four days later General Foch named the now virtually treeless area the "Wood of the Marine Brigade." The 2nd ID took 8,100 casualties during the fighting.

The Memorial consists of a flagpole and a bronze plaque showing a bas-relief of a marine in combat gear surrounded by French 75's. There are also five interpretative panels nearby to explain the Brigade's operations in 1918. GPS: N49 4.407 E3 17.451.

Just outside the gates of the Aisne-Marne ABMC cemetery near Belleau Wood is a small cathedral dedicated to the 26th Infantry Division.

Aisne-Marne American Cemetery

The Aisne-Marne Cemetery occupies at 42.5-acre site just south of the village of Belleau and north of the Belleau Wood where American marines fought the Boche forces advancing on Paris to a standstill in June, 1918. It contains 2,289 burials; the names of another 1,060 missing-in-action are inscribed on the interior walls of the chapel.

The cemetery can be reached from Paris by taking the A4-E50 (Autoroute de l'Est) toward Reims, exiting at Montreuil-aux-Lions (#19) about 21 km short of Chateau-Thierry. Follow the cemetery signs through the village of Lucy-le-Bocage to the Belleau Wood. You enter the cemetery from the north off of D9 along a long tree-lined avenue.

The cathedral on the cemetery grounds was bombed during World War II by an ME-109 Messerschmitt fighter. Several tombstones were destroyed by strafing.

German artillery still stands guard near infantry trenches and a small German WWI cemetery is located a half-kilometer to the northwest off D9. Contact the cemetery at Aisne-Marne

American Cemetery, 02400 Belleau, France. Phone: +33(0) 3 23 70 70 90. GPS coordinates: N49 04.767 E3 17.48.

The Croix Rouge Farm Memorial

This memorial, not far from the old farmhouse so fiercely defended by the Boche, consists of a poignant statue of a doughboy carrying a dead figure. The sculpture is the work of James Butler, whose many impressive works include a bust of the Queen Mother and a moving D-Day memorial to the Green Howards in Normandy. He was commissioned by the Croix Rouge Memorial Association, a group dedicated to keeping alive the memory of the 167th IR.

Destroyed farmhouse at Croix Rouge Farm battlefield site.

Although the memorial is only a short distance north of the A4-E50 autoroute, there is no nearby exit. Driving from Paris, you will have to use exit 20 at Château-Thierry; coming from Reims your exit is 21 (Dormans). Both routes from those exits will take you over small blacktop country roads and through small country towns for considerable distances. Drivers will see frequent signs directing them to the "American monument."

Oise-Aisne American Cemetery

The cemetery contains over 6,000 burials and commemorates another 241 doughboys missing-in-action. A Romanesque-style colonnade inscribed with the names of the missing stands at the head of the cemetery. A chapel and a map room, displaying a color-coded wall map of the nearby AEF military operations, flank the colonnade.

The cemetery is located about 8.5 kilometers north of Château Thierry, just east of the village of Fère-en-Tardenois off highway D2. From Paris, exit the A4-E50 at Château Thierry (exit 20), turn north off the circle on D1, and then drive north toward Soissons. In a little over 6.5 kilometers turn east on D2 toward Fère. The cemetery can also be reached if you are traveling from the east by leaving the A4-E50 at exit 21 and driving north on D2. GPS coordinates: N49 12.134 E3 32.894.

Contact the staff at Oise-Aisne American Cemetery, CD2 02130 Seringes-et-Nesles, France. Phone: +33(0) 3 23 82 21 81.

The Memorial at Oisne-Aisne ABMC Cemetery. The cemetery also features "Plot E" which contains the graves of 96 World War II soldiers convicted of rape, murder, or both. Pvt. Eddie Slovik, the only soldier executed for cowardice in World War II, was buried there until disinterred in 1987.

The Eastern Tour: Day Two and Beyond

Verdun

Verdun is a good place to end the first day of your Eastern tour. To visit the city's WWI sites will take at least a day. From Verdun, it's a reasonable drive south to the St. Mihiel salient or northwest to the Meuse-Argonne sites. Souilly is just across the A4 Autoroute to the south. Chaumont is a much longer drive south; the first 50 km over the Voie Sacrée takes you to Bar-le-Duc. From there it's another 100 kilometers to Chaumont. It's also possible to drive north out of Verdun on D964, up the east side of the Meuse valley, to visit memorials to the 2nd ID, the 316 Infantry (79th ID) and the stele commemorating Pvt. Henry Gunther.

If you are returning to Paris directly from the Meuse-Argonne area, you might consider spending the night in Reims to shorten your trip and visit one of France's most historic cities. The driving distances are not great: from Verdun to Reims is about 121 kilometers and it's another 143 kilometers from Reims to Paris.

Le Mémorial de Verdun

This major WWI museum reopened in 2016 after a recent renovation. Its collection contains artifacts, weapons, uniforms and documents relating to the 1916 battle. Verdun is an essential stop on any tour of WWI sites and Mémorial should not be missed if you are in Verdun. Guided tours of the battlefield are available.

Le Mémorial is open daily from 9:30 a.m. to 5:00 p.m. in winter and from 9:30 to 7:00 in summer. Annual closure runs from December 23 to through the end of January. Admission charged.

For more information go to its website: memorial-verdun.fr. Phone: +33 (0)3 29 84 35 34.

War damage still visible on the famous Reims Cathedral.

Chaumont Marker – AEF Headquarters

The Chaumont Marker is a bronze plaque fastened to the outside front of the old Damrémont Barracks building (to the left of the main gate of what is now L'École de Gendarmerie de Chaumont). It is similar to the First Army Marker in Souilly with the side-by-side text in both English and French: The AEF Headquarters plaque reads:

GENERAL HEADQUARTERS
OF THE
AMERICAN EXPEDITIONARY FORCES
IN EUROPE DURING THE WORLD WAR
OCCUPIED THE BUILDING
OF THE CASERNE DAMRÉMONT
FROM SEPTEMBER 1, 1917
TO MAY 11, 1919
AND FROM HERE
DIRECTED THE ACTIVITIES OF MORE THAN
TWO MILLION AMERICAN SOLDIERS

On July 31, 1917, Pershing and members his staff, including Lt. Col. James G. Harbord and 1st Lt. George S. Patton, Jr., left Paris in two automobiles, a Packard and a Hotchkiss, for an inspection tour of the 1st ID's cantonment at Gondrecourt. A secondary purpose for the long trip to Lorraine was to scout possible locations for the AEF headquarters, then located in Paris' swank Hôtel de Crillon. An advance party had already recommended Chaumont, but Pershing wanted to evaluate the city himself. He found it perfect for the AEF's needs, a small city of about 20,000 inhabitants, far from the social distractions of Paris, but with adequate road and train connections. GHQ moved to Chaumont during the first week of September 1917. GPS coordinates: N48 07.392 E5 08.546.

St. Mihiel Salient Memorials

St. Mihiel American Cemetery

To reach the cemetery from Verdun, take exit 32 off autoroute A4 just past Verdun. Drive south on D904 from Fresnes-en-Woëvre to Thiaucourt.

The cemetery may also be reached from the St. Mihiel Memorial at Montsec by leaving Montsec on D119 to Richecourt, where you pick up D28 northeast to Thiaucourt. Turn west on D3 to the cemetery.

The cemetery fills 40.5 beautifully landscaped acres just west of Thiaucourt- Regniéville off highway D3. It is divided into four equal rectangles, separated by linden trees and paths that contain 4,153 burials. The back of the cemetery is dominated by a peristyle flanked by a chapel and a map room featuring an inlaid marble map illustrating the St. Mihiel offensive. Names of 284 men missing-in-action are inscribed on the walls. Several unusual sculptures are also found on the grounds – the most striking being a stylized eagle marking a sundial at its center and a sculpture of a doughboy, tin hat in hand, standing before a stylized cross with the inscription:

> BLESSED ARE THEY
> THAT HAVE THE HOME LONGING
> FOR THEY SHALL GO HOME

Contact the staff at St. Mihiel American Cemetery, Route de Verdun, 54470 Thiaucourt, France. Phone: +33(0) 3 83 80 01 01. GPS coordinates: N48 57.419 E3 51.184.

Montsec American Monument

The Montsec American Monument is a graceful circular colonnade standing atop the Montsec hill inside the St. Mihiel salient. It commemorates the U.S. First Army's September attack to eliminate the salient. The names of the villages liberated are inscribed on the frieze. The interior of the colonnade is filled with a bronze relief map illustrating First Army's operations.

The Monument can be reached by driving 23 kilometers east from the town of St. Mihiel on D119 to Montsec, and there picking up D12 south to the turnoff that climbs the hill to the colonnade. GPS coordinates: N48 53.40.2 E5 42.803.

5th ID steles (2) off D3 and D958

Both of these steles are small, white stone obelisks bearing the red diamond insignia of the division and small bronze plaques. The first stands about 6 km southeast of Thiaucourt off D3. The plaque also commemorates the passing of the division along this route a second time in 1944. The second stele is about 2.5 km south of the first as the crow flies. To reach it from the first you need to continue on D3 southeast until it intersects with D958, where you turn east on D598 to the second stele. The two steles are virtually identical, except for the bronze plaques. The drive is relatively short from the American Cemetery outside Thiaucourt.

Pershing inserted the 5th ID in the line between the 2nd and the 90th IDs for the drive north.

Souilly

1st Army Headquarters plaque

Souilly is a small town on the Voie Sacrée, now N35, the road that so many tens of thousands of French *poilus* traveled from the railhead at Bar-le-Duc to the killing fields at Verdun in 1916, never to return. Markers along the roadside trace this sacred way to remember their deaths.

The ABMC had this heavily weathered bronze tablet originally attached to a wall of the Souilly Mairie (town hall) to mark the building because it was used as the First Army HQ. The inscription, in the shape of an urn, reads in English (the French version alongside it):

> THE HEADQUARTERS
> OF THE AMERICAN FIRST ARMY
> OCCUPIED THIS BUILDING
> FROM SEPTEMBER 21, 1918
> TO THE END OF HOSTILITIES,
> AND FROM HERE CONDUCTED
> THE MEUSE-ARGONNE OFFENSIVE
> ONE OF THE GREAT OPERATIONS
> OF THE WORLD WAR
> ERECTED BY
> UNITED STATES OF AMERICA

The inscription tells most of the story. Pétain had his HQ in this building during the siege of Verdun in 1916. Pershing and his staff made a point of visiting Verdun during their move from Chaumont to Souilly to pay their respects to the French sacrifice. Pershing kept his private train at a nearby siding during the Meuse-Argonne offensive, although it doesn't appear that he used it other than to entertain visitors.

To reach Souilly and travel a portion of the Voie Sacrée, exit the A4-E50 autoroute at Verdun (exit 30), and then drive a short distance south on N35. GPS coordinates: N49 01.685 E17.159.

Meuse-Argonne Battlefield Memorials

Varennes-en-Argonne:

State of Missouri Memorial

A memorial to the doughboys from Missouri stands off D 38, just outside Varennes. It is one of those battlefield monuments that was erected outside the jurisdiction of the ABMC.

Missouri Monument set against a French sky.

The Museum of Mine Warfare

The small museum contains American artifacts, including some Harry S. Truman mementos.

Meuse-Argonne American Cemetery

The 130.5 acre Meuse-Argonne Cemetery, with 14, 246 burials, is the largest American military cemetery in Europe. The grave markers stand in neat rows in rectangular spaces formed by hedges. There is the usual graceful chapel flanked by loggias at the far end.

A bronze screen divides the chapel, and its interior is decorated with stained-glass windows decorated with the insignia of the American units that fought nearby. The loggias display maps of the Meuse-Argonne offensive and the names of 954 Americans whose bodies were not recovered are inscribed on the Tablets of the Missing, including a number who died in our Russian intervention in 1918-19.

The cemetery is located just outside the village of Romagne-sous-Montfaucon, north of Varennes-en-Argonne. The route is signed.

Contact the staff at Meuse-Argonne American Cemetery, Rue du Général Pershing, 55110 Romagne-sous-Montfaucon, France. Phone: +33(0) 3 24 85 14 18. GPS coordinates: N49 20.044 E5 05.376.

Despite being the largest U.S. Cemetery in Europe, only a few hundred visit it each year. A new visitor's center is being constructed. In World War II, the Germans put an anti-aircraft position on the hill adjacent to the cemetery, resulting in the cemetery being bombed and strafed by the U.S. Army Air Corps.

Montfaucon American Monument

This imposing, grandiose 200 ft. high, Doric column is located about 11 km south of the Meuse-Argonne American Cemetery atop Montfaucon.

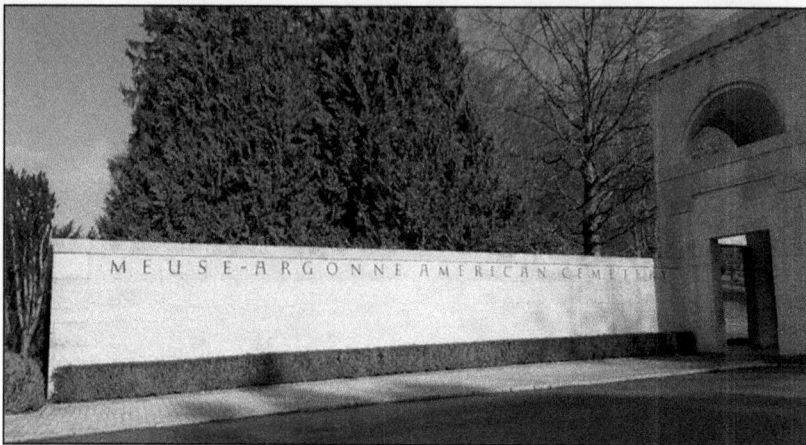

The column is surmounted by a female figure representing the American victory in the Meuse-Argonne offensive. The column is hollow and a staircase (234 steps) leads to an observation platform giving the hardy climber a magnificent view of the battlefield. The walls of the foyer are inscribed with a map of the campaign and various inscriptions. It was dedicated by the ABMC in 1937 and designed by John Russell Pope, one of the chief public monuments architects of the day, who also gave us both the Jefferson Memorial and the west wing of the National Gallery. President Franklin D. Roosevelt spoke at the dedication via a radio address.

The Monument is open during the warmer months from 9 a.m. to 9 p.m. daily; from October through April, it is open 9 a.m. to 5 p.m. on Friday, Saturday and Sunday.

It's located in a wood on the eastern outskirts of the village of Montfaucon d'Argonne, about 10 km on D19 from Varennes-en-Argonne. GPS coordinates: N49 16.354 E5 08.519.

Montfaucon Monument sits eerily on top of a commanding hill.

Other American monuments on the Meuse-Argonne battlefield Nantillois and vicinity

To reach Nantillois, drive north from Montfaucon for 4.5 km on D 15. In the village itself, there is a stately non-ABMC memorial to the doughboys from Pennsylvania that consists of a low stone wall inscribed with the words:

"WHO SERVED IN THE GREAT WAR."

Only part of the massive Pennsylvania Monument, dedicated in 1927, in Varrenes-en-Argonne.

A plaque to the "glorious dead of the 315th Infantry, USA" is fastened to the side of the Nantillois Community Center, a building that veterans of the 315th Infantry (79th ID) built for the town after the war.

Also, there is a stone stele, memorializing the dead of the 317th Infantry that was dedicated outside Nantillois in defiance of the wishes of Gen. Pershing, then head of the ABMC.

A 4th Division Monument, consisting of a stele, is located north of Nantillois off D 15.

Sites of The Lost Battalion stand and of Sgt. Alvin York's attack.

Driving directions to these locations are at the end of Appendix I below.

Sommepy American Monument, Sommepy-Tahure

The Sommepy monument is located apart from the other Meuse-Argonne sites because it was erected to commemorate the American units that served with the Fourth French Army west of the Argonne Forest. The monument, which is three miles northwest of the village of Sommepy-Tahure, stands atop of the Blanc Mont ridge, a key German defensive position between Reims and the Argonne Forest. New York architect Arthur Loomis Harmon designed it as a square tower made of sandstone blocks with an observation platform on top, strongly resembling a medieval keep. The outside walls carry plaques to the American infantry units that fought in the vicinity beginning with the 42nd ID in July, the 2nd ID and three regiments (369th, 371st and 372nd) of the 93rd ID at the beginning of the Meuse-Argonne offensive in late September and the 36th ID until late October. There are plaques in the foyer that interpret the operations of these units.

The monument front displays a spread eagle with the inscription in English and French:

ERECTED BY THE UNITED STATES OF AMERICA TO
COMMEMORATE THE ACHIEVEMENTS OF HER
SOLDIERS
AND THOSE OF FRANCE WHO FOUGHT IN THIS REGION
DURING THE GREAT WAR.

The outside walls bear plaques commemorating the individual American units.

The Sommepy Mairie contains a memorial room that details the reconstruction of the village after the war.

The monument is open in the summer from 9 a.m. to 5 p.m. on weekdays and 9 a.m. to 6 p.m. on weekends. Phone: +33(0)3 29 85 14 18. GPS coordinates: N49 17.047 E4 32.174.

Trench lines still scar Sommepy to show defensive lines.

East Bank of the Meuse Battlefield Memorials
In order to visit the memorials on the east bank of the Meuse, leave Verdun by D 964. Your drive north will take you along the river valley with the Heights of the Meuse looming on your right. On your way north, you will pass by the riverside towns of Dun-sur-Meuse and Brieulles where the 5th and 32nd IDs of the III Corps forced crossings in early November.

Pvt. Henry Gunther memorial stele, Chaumont-devant-Damvillers
This simple stone memorial with an American flag flying over it commemorates the last doughboy officially to die in France before the Armistice went into effect. The memorial is maintained by the people of Chaumont to honor the men of the 313th Infantry who liberated the village.

Chaumont is located 17.4 km east of Consenvoye (on D 964) by a tortuous road. The stele is about a kilometer north of the village. Coordinates: N49 18 55.69 E5 25 45.14.

The 316th Infantry Memorial, Sivry-sur-Meuse

In 23 kilometers you will reach the town of Sivry-sur-Meuse. There, take a hard right, leaving town by the Rue Pierre Pinton. In 1.25 miles, turn north (left) on a farm road then, in another half-mile turn right and drive to the Memorial's tree-lined entrance road.

The Memorial consists of an impressive square, ornate white-stone column with inscriptions on all sides in English and French describing the battle history of the regiment. This is one of the 79th ID's memorials built despite the objections of the retired Gen. Pershing, then head of the ABMC. Coordinates: N49 19 42.63 E 5 18 36.60.

V Corps and 2nd ID Markers

From Sivry drive north along D964 to Moulins-Saint-Hubert (35.5 km.). About 2km. beyond Sivry, you will pass two memorials, one squat cemented stone block with a plaque memorializing the V Corps, whose 2nd ID marines made a night crossing the Meuse near here. A second commemorative 2nd ID boulder-marker is nearby if you continue north for another 2 km.

If you decide to explore the monuments and the American cemetery to the west, there is a bridge crossing the Meuse at Mouzon, a couple of kilometers farther north on D964.

German trench lines still visible at Sommepy Memorial.

APPENDICES

I. Two Soldiers in the Argonne Forest: Charles W. Whittlesey and Alvin C. York

The Meuse-Argonne offensive has left us with two incidents that still resonate in the American memory of the Great War – the saga of the "Lost Battalion" and the legend of Sgt. Alvin C. York. Yet, ask most Baby Boomers or Millennials today about those incidents and you will probably only elicit a vague reply or a blank stare. American history textbooks no longer spend much time with the details of military operations or heroes, preferring instead to dwell on impersonal social and economic issues. It strikes the authors that brief accounts of the actions of these two remarkable citizen-soldiers will enable the traveler to visit their personal battlefields with an appreciation of their heroism.

Maj. Charles W. Whittlesey, his "Lost Battalion" and the burden of military command:

Ever since the survivors of Maj. Charles W. Whittlesey's "Lost Battalion" walked away from their funkholes in the Argonne Forest on October 7, they, along with future historians, have stated to anyone who would pay attention that they were neither a battalion nor lost. No matter, the name that reporters fastened on them at the time has stuck for the past century.

The brief summary we present here is based on what historians today believe happened along the Charlevaux Brook from October 2-7, 1918 in the midst of the First Army's Meuse-Argonne campaign.

Charles White Whittlesey was born in Wisconsin in 1884, but sometime later his family moved to Massachusetts where he graduated from Pittsfield High School and Williams College. With his Williams degree in hand, he moved easily to Harvard University, where he received his law degree in 1908 and partnered with a Harvard classmate opening a law practice in New York City. After a brief flirtation with the American Socialist party, Whittlesey got caught up in the preparedness movement in 1914, even to the point of attending the officer-training program at Plattsburgh, N.Y. That summer's military training qualified him for an Army commission when he left his law firm in May 1917 to enlist in the Army. The newly-minted captain was assigned to the 77th ID, largely drafted from New York's City's Lower East Side. Its members were reputed to have spoken 42 different languages, so one can only wonder how they coped with the officers who commanded them or, for that matter, the "limeys" who later trained them.

By September 1918, the 77th ID had gained a great deal of combat experience while holding a section of the trenches along the Vesle River. Replacements had eroded the New York character of the division, as many of the new men were from western states. On the Vesle, one assumes, the New Yorkers had become reasonably proficient with their rifles since a staff study found that as many as 45% of the doughboys in two of the 77th's regiments had never fired them in training. Whatever the case, in September, the division occupied the far left of the First Army line, directly in front of the rugged Argonne Forest for the upcoming offensive.

Thus, on October 2, "Galloping Charlie," the not-so-flattering nickname accorded the newly promoted major, found himself leading a mixed force – seven companies from two different battalions and two machine gun sections, some 554 men all told, part of the 308th Infantry – in an attack through a gap in the German lines deep in the Argonne Forest. He did so in full expectation that his move would be supported on his left flank by the French Fourth Army, also participating in the advance, and on his right by the American 28th ID. As ordered, Whittlesey advanced to his objective, a road running along the north side of a stream to the Charlevaux Mill, but then decided that maintaining such an exposed position during the night would be foolish, so he ordered his men to dig in along the wooded creek bottom where they would be better protected from German artillery fire. All might have been well had the flanking units also advanced that day, but they had not. As night fell on the 2nd, Whittlesey's "battalion" found itself stranded about a half-mile inside German lines, a threat to their entire defensive line.

Whittlesey dropped off a squad on his advance to act as runners and he had six homing pigeons with him, so it is doubtful that he was overly worried at first about communicating with his superiors and there was no reason for him to believe that the Germans wouldn't pull back when the French and American divisions on his flanks moved forward. Both he and his second in command, Capt. George G. McMurtry, felt bound by a written order from their division commander, Maj. Gen. Robert Alexander, that "ground once captured must under no circumstances be given up" without positive orders from his HQ. So, Whittlesey elected to hold his ground rather than attempt a fighting retreat. It turned out to be a bad decision no matter how rational it might have seemed at the moment. For some still inexplicable reason, neither Alexander nor his superiors were able to organize a successful attack to rescue Whittlesey's beleaguered men. Instead, it took a daring flanking movement by the 82nd ID, miles to the east, designed primarily to relieve pressure on the 1st ID, to force the Germans to retreat. It wasn't that the "Lost Battalion's" plight was unknown. Whittlesey sent out a homing pigeon every day of the siege and reporters immediately began to file stories in which they fastened the name "Lost Battalion" on his command.

In the five days and nights before the Germans pulled back, they kept up a constant attack on the Americans. Numerous times grenadiers charged down the 200-foot high stream bank, lobbing potato-masher grenades ahead of them, hoping to overrun the defenders. Each time, the half-starved riflemen calmly picked off the charging *Soldaten*, driving them back in confusion. Repeatedly the doughboys, hunkered down in their funkholes, were hit by arching-fire from a huge trench mortar that they were unable to neutralize. Before the siege was lifted, the Boche had called up a flamethrower team to add terror to their incessant attacks. Eventually, the mortar, machine gun, sniper and artillery fire took their toll: food ran out; ammo supplies were low; water could only be secured from the Charlevaux at night; attempts at resupply from the air failed miserably; the position was hit by friendly artillery fire, and there was no way to adequately care for the wounded or bury the dead. Stench alone made the Lost Battalion's position intolerable. All the while, Whittlesey, McMurtry, both wounded, and Capt. Nelson M. Holderman, commanding K Company, moved among the funkholes encouraging their men to hold out until relieved.

With the men muttering about slipping away on their own at night, Whittlesey faced a command decision of an almost unbearable moral dimension when the besieging Germans presented him with a typed note, written in English by *Hauptmann* Fritz Prinz, who had once lived in Seattle, pleading for him to surrender what was left of his command in the name of humanity. But, the lanky, bespectacled major, the by-the-book commander, backed by McMurtry, refused the German demand. When men from the 307th IR relieved the Lost Battalion a day later, Whittlesey was able to lead only 194 out of his original 554 men out of the ravine. The others were either dead or too wounded to walk.

At one desperate moment when his position was coming under friendly fire, his runner-posts long before eliminated, Whittlesey sent out his last homing pigeon with his coordinates and a plea that the American batteries ceasefire. "We are along the road Parallel 276.4," he scribbled, "Our own artillery is dropping a barrage directly on us. For heaven's sake, stop it." The pigeon, "Cher Ami," made it back to her coop although wounded severely enough to require an artificial leg. She survived the war and was brought back to Fort Monmouth, N.J. where she died on June 13, 1919. This remarkable pigeon, mounted by a taxidermist, was given to the Smithsonian Institute where she resides today. (Cher Ami and Comanche, Capt. Miles Keogh's mount that survived the Battle of the Little Bighorn (1876), now on display at the University of Kansas Museum, participants in two of the U.S. Army's most famous battles, are still with us today in their actual, once-living mantles.)

For their exceptional courage during the siege, Whittlesey McMurtry and Holderman received Medals of Honor. All three were pallbearers at the dedication of the Tomb of the Unknowns three years later.

In 1919, the Army convened a court-martial board in France to hear charges brought against a Lt. Maurice Revnes, an officer in the 306th Machine-Gun Battalion, who had suggested that Whittlesey negotiate with the Germans over an exchange of the wounded – a suggestion that Whittlesey and McMurtry rejected. By the time the case was heard in France, Whittlesey was in United States, recently promoted to Lieutenant Colonel and a Medal of Honor recipient. Since the GHQ declined to send him back to France for the court-martial, the proceedings went on without his testimony. The three-day trial thus became an inquiry into Whittlesey's decisions during the siege. Revnes was easily acquitted because of his personal bravery, but a shadow was cast over his commanding officer's judgment.

Whittlesey, back at his law firm, besieged by his former men needing financial help and probably suffering from what we now term "post traumatic stress disorder," broke under the strain of adjusting to peacetime life. He apparently committed suicide by jumping from the deck of a Havana-bound United Fruit steamer in November 1921, just a few days after serving as a pallbearer at the dedication ceremony in Arlington.

Whittlesey was not alone among veterans suffering from PTSD. It was estimated by the American Legion that as many as two former doughboys committed suicide every day throughout the 1920s and beyond; the price of victory has always been borne by those men who fought to win that victory.

Whittlesey is remembered today by a cenotaph in a Pittsfield, Mass. cemetery and by a collection of memorabilia, including his helmet and the surrender request from *Hauptmann* Prinz, at Williams College in Williamstown, Mass.

Finding the "Lost Battalion" today:

Although the actual site of the Lost Battalion's stand is still remote and roadless, it is possible to drive to its proximity. There are three memorials near the site – one in the village of Binarville just west of D 63 as it runs through the village; the other two are at either end of the Charlevaux reservoir.

Probably the most direct route to the memorials is to drive the A-4 from Paris to the Dommartin-Dampierre exit, and then take D3 north to Sainte-Menehould. From there, pick up D 63 to Binarville. While driving through Binarville, you will pass a building with a number of plaques relating to the "Lost Battalion." To reach the other two memorial plaques, continue north out of Binarville a short distance before veering right onto

D66. The first memorial you reach is a modernistic stone stele standing above a number of WWI style helmets on one of which Cher Ami is perched. It stands by the highway just before you reach two farm complexes and the reservoir. The second memorial stele is also located off D66 just beyond the east end of the reservoir. On one side is the simple inscription "Lost Battalion" with an arrow pointing down the hillside. The reverse side lists the hodgepodge of AEF units that Whittlesey commanded in the pocket.

To visit the village of Châtel-Chéhéry and the Sgt. York memorials from the "Lost Battalion" sites continue east on D66 for about 7 km. (After a short distance D66 becomes D442.) Along D442, just outside Apremont, you will pass a German WWI cemetery, the bleakness of which stands in sharp contrast to the American WWI cemeteries. In Apremont, take D42 northwest a little over 2 km to Châtel-Chéhéry.

Sgt. Alvin C. York and the morality of military service:

Alvin C. York, native of Pall Mall Tenn., will always be remembered as "Sgt. York," although he was only a newly-promoted corporal when he performed his martial feats during the Meuse-Argonne offensive, and 50 years later died holding the rank of colonel in both Army Signal Corps and the Tennessee National Guard. Regardless, it is as the unlettered "Sgt. York" that Alvin entered into the pantheon of American military heroes.

Alvin York, as the cliché has had it for a century, was an American original. After a hard-drinking, carousing adolescence, he found Jesus and soon morphed into an intensely religious pacifist. So, when war was declared, Alvin initially applied for status as a conscientious objector. His request was denied and, while his appeal was being heard, the Army shipped him out to Camp Gordon, Ga. to become a cog in the draftee 82nd ID.

There, he ran into two persuasive officers, Maj. Gonzalo Buxton and Capt. Edward Danforth, who used his own book, the Holy Bible, to wean him from his pacifism and convince him of the morality of the war into which he was about to be thrust.

Alvin York aboard the *USS Ohioan* en route home after the war (Photo: Wikimedia)

Skip ahead to the morning of October 8, when the 328th Infantry, 82nd ID of which York's Company C was a part, found itself attacking northwest out of Châtel-Chéhéry into the hills west of the Aire River to relieve pressure on the 1st ID and Whittlesey's "Lost Battalion." The immediate objective of the 328th's attack was a north-south supply road (along with a small rail line paralleling it) that ran a little over a mile west of the village, which constituted major supply routes for German forces holding the Argonne Forest.

On October 7 the German 2nd Württemberg Landwehr Division, consisting of the 120th, 122nd and 125th Regiments, had moved to the eastern edge of the Argonne to protect those supply routes, taking up positions astride a valley that ran west from Châtel-Chéhéry. *Leutnant* Paul Vollmer, known to his friends as "Kuno," the pre-war assistant-postmaster of Ulm, commanded the 1st Battalion of the 120th Regiment that was tasked with stopping any further Yank advance into the threatened area.

Meanwhile in the fighting on October 7, the 1st Battalion of the 328th Infantry had gained, and then lost, most of Hill 223 (Castle Hill) just north of Châtel-Chéhéry. York's 2nd Battalion was now tasked with continuing the drive by attacking through the decimated 1st Battalion the next morning. That advance would put the doughboys squarely in the sights of Vollmer's machine guns.

The German tactical plan was to stop the American advance cold on the 8th, before launching a counterattack with the 210th and 212th Regiments of the Prussian Reserve Infantry that were due to arrive on the battlefield in mid-morning.

The American attack kicked off on schedule at 05:00, but was immediately pinned down by machine gun fire coming from a well-fortified hill in the valley center known to the German defenders as the Humserberg. Acting Sgt. Bernard Early received orders to take four squads, totaling 17 men, in a scout south and then west in an effort to outflank the guns. Cpl. York led one of those squads. Undetected, Early's group eventually found a gap in the German line before turning north in a dry ditch they believed would take them into the rear of the German firing positions. As they crept along, they surprised two *Soldaten* filling canteens from a stream. The terrified Krauts spotted the oncoming doughboys, dropped their canteens, and sprinted toward their command post, shouting that the Americans were coming. A decade later, York later described the scene best: "They jumped out of the brush in front of us and run like two scared rabbits. We called them to surrender, and one of our boys done fired and missed. And they kept on a-going. And we kept on after them." This pell-mell rush took the Yanks right into *Leutnant* Vollmer's headquarters. Surprised and thinking that Early's men were the vanguard of a much larger American force, Vollmer surrendered the *Soldaten* under his immediate command.

Monument to Sgt. York in Châtel-Chéhéry dedicated by Tennessee Historical Commission.

But, the real fight had not yet begun. Commanding a machine gun nest on the hillside above Vollmer's HQ, *Leutnant* Paul Lipp saw what had happened, trained his gun around and shouted for all the *Soldaten* to go to ground. When they did so, he opened fire on the still standing Americans, killing six outright and wounding three (killing a number of *Soldaten* as well). Sgt. Early was seriously wounded. One of the dead doughboys was York's best friend, Cpl. Murray Savage, whose body was mangled beyond recognition by a machine gun burst. The gory sight of Savage's corpse provided all the motivation Alvin York needed to take command of the situation. Now the senior noncom, York left his remaining men to guard the prisoners, while he took on the machine guns, backed up, it's now believed, by Pvt. Percy Beardsley who carried a Chauchat automatic rifle.

After climbing up the hillside, York found himself at the intersection of two sunken roads giving him clear lines of fire toward a machine gun position about 50 or 60 yards away. "And those machine guns were spitting fire and cutting down the undergrowth all around me something awful," he recollected later. "As soon as those machine guns opened fire on me, I began to exchange shots with them. There were over thirty of them ... and all I could do was touch the Germans off just as fast as I could. ... All the time I kept yelling at them to come down. I didn't want to kill any more than I had to. But it was they or I. And I was giving them the best I had." When asked a few hours later by Gen. George B. Duncan, the 82nd's CO, how many he had hit, York replied, "General, I would hate to think I missed any of them shots; they were all at pretty close range — 50 or 60 yards." Dropping to the ground, habitually using his wet thumb to clear the front sight, York fired nearly 50 rounds from his Lee-Enfield, killing 19 of the gunners and supporting riflemen. He then started back down the hillside to check on his men and their prisoners.

The nearest town to Sgt. York's famous fight. Most sights are well-marked in the town, but no gasoline!

At that point, a Landwehr officer, *Leutnant* Fritz Endriss spotted him and quickly ordered a dozen *Soldaten* to follow him in a bayonet charge aimed at putting an end to York's rampage. His Lee-Enfield apparently empty, the intrepid corporal dropped to the ground, drew his M1911 .45 pistol and shot six of the charging Germans, *Leutnant* Endriss being last, at a range of about two yards; the rest turned tail. (We now know today from archeological evidence presented by author/biographer, Douglas V. Mastriano, that there was a second shooter firing a .45 on the hillside that morning, most likely Mastriano thinks, Pvt. Percy Beardsley.)

A short time later, Vollmer, very likely shaken by the sight of his friend Endriss, gut shot, screaming as he fell to the ground, convinced *Leutnant* Paul Lipp of the 125th Regiment to surrender the remainder of his command to York as well. With their 130 plus prisoners in a column of twos, led by the three surrendered German officers, York walking directly behind them with his .45 drawn, the eight surviving Americans then marched their prisoners back along their morning's route into Châtel-Chéhéry.

York can be seen between the left and center German officers as he marches his prisoners into Châtel- Chéhéry. (Photo: Roy Coles collection, USAHEC)

There was no German counterattack that morning and the German commander, Gen. Max von Gallwitz, his main supply route compromised, soon ordered a general withdrawal from the Argonne.

A final tally estimated that York had personally shot at least 28 of the enemy; he and the survivors of his squad captured 30 plus machine guns and brought in 132 prisoners. Soon after Alvin was awarded the Distinguished Service Cross, which later, after a post-war visit to the battle site, was upgraded to the Medal of Honor. Sometime after that, when presenting him with the French Croix de Guerre and Legion of Honor, Marshal Foch told the newly-promoted sergeant that what he had done "was the greatest thing ever accomplished by any soldier by any of the armies of Europe." When the final tally was complete, York had been awarded nearly 50 medals for his actions in the Argonne. For the remainder of his life he attributed it all to divine intervention, that his having come through the war unscathed was due to his belief that God would protect him so long as his faith was absolute.

In reality, there were other instances in the AEF where doughboys brought in gaggles of surrendered Germans, but none reached the epic level of Alvin York's remarkable feat.

Unlike the saga of the "Lost Battalion" that was known to the American public almost immediately, York's exploits were not widely known until "The Saturday Evening Post" published a version of the story by George Pattullo, "The Second Elder Gives Battle," in its April 26, 1919 issue. That account, distributed to the magazine's two million readers, set the interpretative framework and ensured York a hero's welcome when he arrived back in the U.S. that included a New York City ticker tape parade and an appearance in the House gallery in Washington. A week after returning home to Pall Mall, York married Gracie Loretta Williams (always "Miss Gracie" to Alvin) and the two began a family that in time reached eight. A modest man, York refused to profit from his exploits, finally accepting one gift, a 400-acre farm from the Rotary Club of Nashville that ended up landing him in debt. And, he never forgot his fellow company mates who supported him on that hillside west of Châtel-Chéhéry.

A year after his return from France, he formed the Alvin C. York Foundation to increase educational opportunities in the Cumberland River valley. That effort embroiled him in controversy with state and local education officials, leading to his eventual ouster as president of his own Foundation in 1936. Following that fiasco, he worked as a superintendent for the Civilian Conservation Corps. When the U.S. entered World War II, a decision that he had openly advocated, Alvin attempted to re-enlist, but was denied because of health reasons. However, the Army found a niche for their idle hero by commissioning him in the Signal Corps as a major with the job of touring Army bases, participating in war bond drives and raising money for the Red Cross. He also allowed Howard Hawks to produce a film version of his life, "Sergeant York" (actor Gary Cooper portraying Alvin) that was nominated for 11 Academy Awards, won two and was the highest grossing film of 1941. Alvin earned about $150,000 from film royalties that caused him no end of tax problems, but enabled him to open his long-planned Bible school.

Alvin York suffered a number of strokes in the mid-1950s, remaining bedridden until his death in the VA Hospital in Nashville on September 2, 1964. His funeral service took place in the same Pall Mall church where he had found Jesus 50 years before.

Alvin York Memorials:

Sgt. Alvin C. York State Historical Park, Pall Mall, Tenn.:

The State of Tennessee maintains a small park in Pall Mall, York's hometown, to honor his memory. The park contains a visitor center modeled after the York General Store, the York home, a gristmill, a small museum and a recreation of a WWI trench. Nearby are York's Bible School and the Wolf River Cemetery where Alvin and Miss Gracie are buried. Also nearby is the Wolf River Methodist Church where Alvin had his conversion experience and from where he was buried.

The Park is open daily with 45-minute tours being conducted at 9 a.m., 10 a.m., 11 a.m., 1 p.m., 2 p.m. and 3 p.m. There is a small charge for the tour.

Pall Mall is located in the northeastern corner of Tennessee, 47 miles north of the Crossville exit on I-40.

Sgt. Alvin C. York Statue:

A statue of York standing while sighting down the barrel of his Lee-Enfield rifle is located on the Tennessee State capitol grounds in Nashville.

York Battle Site Tour:

Over the years the exact location of Alvin York's exploits became lost, other than it was somewhere west of the village of Châtel-Chéhéry. A decade ago, surveys by Douglas Mastriano located the sites and a trail was created for visitors in 2007-08. The "Circuit de Sergeant York" runs from the village westward making a 2 km-loop. At the top of the loop there is a small park with an orientation board. A number of trail signs mark the way.

There is also a stone memorial along highway D42 as it runs through the village that commemorates York.

II. The Spanish Flu and the AEF

Often overlooked today is the fact that the worst infectious disease pandemic the world has ever experienced, the so-called "Spanish flu," struck right at the end of the World War, 1917-1918. Despite a century of "on and off 'investigation, there is no real consensus as to its origin or scope, only that it was a worldwide disaster of a magnitude never before or since recorded. Over two years, variant strains of the H1N1 influenza virus infected an estimated 500 million people in every corner of the globe. In three successive waves it carried off three to five percent of the world's population, thereby lowering worldwide life expectancy by 12 percent. It struck especially hard in the ranks of the often-undernourished soldiers fighting on the Western Front, packed as they were in training camps, troopships and muddy, rat-infested trenches.

The Spanish flu, of course, did not originate in Spain, but, because of Spain's neutrality, reporters there were freer to file stories about the pandemic, that name stuck. Nor is there any consensus today about its origins. One recent researcher thinks the virus first appeared in a remote, southwestern Kansas county in 1917, spreading to training camps and then to Europe with the influx of doughboys. Others think it may have had its origin in the Far East and been brought to Europe by Chinese and Vietnamese soldiers serving as auxiliaries in the British and French armies. Another study traced its movement from the Far East through Boston to debarkation centers in France to the combatants. From Europe and North America the disease apparently spread via ship to all parts of the globe.

We do know that the virus struck in three waves – its first iteration in 1917 caused debilitating illness, but the mortality rate was normal and the virus attacked mature adults. The second wave that appeared in September, and lasted through the end of the year, was apparently a more virulent H1N1 mutation. The death rate spiked worldwide. A third appearance of the flu virus came in the first half of 1919 was a milder form, following the normal virus mutation pattern. While the influenza virus itself could kill, most deaths occurred from pneumonia, a secondary bacterial infection.

The effect of the pandemic on the war effort was profound. The first wave sickened inductees in 24 training camps, convalescence lasting a week and full recovery a couple more. The second, killer wave apparently first appeared aboard a naval receiving ship tied up at Boston in late August. From there it spread throughout the nation infecting millions of civilians, killing maybe 500,000. Selective Service suspended draft calls and training went by the wayside, maybe a reason why so many doughboys arrived in France without having fired a rifle. Forty percent of the inductees (13,161) at Camp Sherman near Chillicothe, Ohio came down with the flu in late September; fatalities numbered 1,101 of the infected, illustrating the fact that the new, deadly mutation had a special affinity for the young and previously healthy. AEF soldiers already in France were less seriously affected, probably because of an acquired immunity, still 12,423 doughboys died overseas in 1918. The total number of deaths in the AEF from the flu is estimated at about 25,000, with another 360,000 becoming seriously ill. Combat deaths are estimated at 53,402.

The Navy lost 5,027 seamen to the flu in 1918, twice the number of combat fatalities. Along with the sailors, doughboys sickened and died on troop transports while crossing the Atlantic. The effect of the pandemic on the undernourished soldiers and civilians of the German Empire was catastrophic.

This pandemic had run its course by the end of 1919, but as we know today, the influenza viruses are still out there and continue to reappear periodically with devastating consequences.

III. Battlefield Memorials Not Maintained By The American Battlefield Monuments Commission

After the war, many veterans who had fought on the battlefields of France wished to have that world-changing experience commemorated, thus they began almost immediately to erect memorials near where they had fought and many of their buddies had died. In addition, American cities and states, various French municipalities, plus organizations such as the American Red Cross, erected memorials commemorating the participation of their citizens or employees (or their gratitude for American aid) in the Great War. By the time the ABMC published its updated guide to the battlefields, "American Armies and Battlefields in Europe," in 1938, the number had risen to 91, all of which are detailed in its "Chapter XV, Miscellaneous" and reproduced below. They range from a stone tower standing on a lonely headland on the Isle of Islay, Scotland, commemorating those soldiers and sailors lost when the S.S. *Tuscania* was torpedoed by U-77 to a stained-glass window in the church at Semur-en-Auxois, far from the Western Front, donated by the 310th Infantry.

Recently, new memorials have been dedicated, most notably the 28th Infantry's memorial in Cantigny (2008) and the statue placed at the Croix Rouge Farm north of Château-Thierry by the Croix Rouge Memorial Foundation to honor the 167th Infantry (42nd "Rainbow" ID) in 2011. Undoubtedly, more memorials will be dedicated in the next few years during the Centenary.

The 1938 list of memorials is found on the following pages:

AMERICAN WORLD WAR MEMORIALS IN EUROPE ERECTED BY AGENCIES OTHER THAN THE UNITED STATES GOVERNMENT

IN addition to the memorials erected by the United States Government there are a number of other American World War memorials in Europe. Some of these were in existence before the American Battle Monuments Commission was created and others are useful memorials constructed with the Commission's approval. A few are memorials to American units which served with the French Army before the United States entered the war and concerning the erection of which the Commission was without jurisdiction.

For the benefit of those interested there is given below a tabulation of American World War commemorative memorials in Europe of which the American Battle Monuments Commission has a record and which were erected by agencies other than those of the United States Government.

This table does not include monuments to units smaller than a regiment, markers now falling to pieces, French village monuments which commemorate American units in addition to their own dead, and monuments to foreign armies erected by Americans or from American sources.

In this connection it may be stated that the Commission feels that the memorial project of the United States Government, described in Chapter XII, adequately commemorates all units of the American forces in Europe during the World War and that the erection of any additional American monuments abroad would not be in good taste and should be prohibited.

Unit or event commemorated	Number	Location	Character	Date erected	Remarks
V Corps	1	3 miles southeast of Mouzon (Ardennes) on the main road.	Small marker built of field stones.	Soon after the Armistice.	Erected by members of unit to mark V Corps line at the Armistice. See picture, page 301.
1st Division	5	(a) Along road ⅓ mile southeast of Cantigny (Somme). (b) On main highway west of Buzancy (Aisne). (c) At road junction east of Vigneulles (Meuse). (d) Along main road ½ mile east of St. Juvin (Ardennes). (e) Along road south of Wadelincourt (Ardennes).	Small concrete shaft, surmounted by a carved eagle of stone.	1919	Erected by the 1st Div. Names of dead in vicinity given on bronze plates. See picture on page 521.
2d Division	22	On all of the battlefields where the division had fighting.	Concrete boulder about 3 feet in diameter, with 2d Div. insignia in bronze upon it.	Soon after the Armistice.	Erected by men from the division. See picture on page 520.
3d Division	1	Château-Thierry (Aisne), northwest of the main bridge.	Stone monument of medium size.	1923	Erected by division to its deeds and dead. See picture, page 60.

MISCELLANEOUS   523

Unit or event commemorated	Number	Location	Character	Date erected	Remarks
4th Division	3	(a) About 1 mile west of Fismes (Marne). (b) At the eastern exit of Manheulles (Meuse). (c) About 1 mile west of town of Brieulles-sur-Meuse.	Small stone obelisk.	Soon after the Armistice.	Erected by the division. See the picture appearing on page 80.
5th Division	28	On all of the battlefields where the division had fighting.	Small obelisk of concrete.	Soon after the Armistice.	Erected by men of the division. Inscriptions give details of fighting. See picture on page 525.
5th Division	1	Dun-sur-Meuse	An ornamental wrought-iron railing on a bridge.	1932	Erected by the 5th Div. Assn. to commemorate crossing of the Meuse River.
26th Division	1	Belleau (Aisne)	Reconstruction of village church.	1929	Erected by the 26th Div. Assn. in memory of division's dead. See picture, page 53.
28th Division	1	Fismes (Marne)	Ornamental stone bridge.	1927	Erected by the State of Pennsylvania. See picture, page 525.
30th Division	1	Along the main road south of town of Bellicourt (Aisne).	Small monument of cut stone.	1923	Erected by the State of Tennessee to her troops of the 59th and 60th Brigades. See picture, page 377.
37th Division	1	Montfaucon (Meuse).	Substantial stone building, donated for use as an almshouse.	1929	Erected by the State of Ohio. See picture of building on page 214.
37th Division	1	Eyne, Belgium	A large bridge, stucco finish.	1929	Erected by the State of Ohio to commemorate crossing of Escaut River by 37th Division. See the picture on page 397.
80th Division	1	Nantillois (Meuse)	Medium-size stone fountain.	1927	Erected by the State of Pennsylvania. See picture on page 525.
102d Infantry (26th Division.)	1	Seicheprey (Meurthe-et-Moselle).	Small granite fountain (no water).	1923	Presented by men and women of the State of Connecticut. See picture on page 128.
117th Infantry (30th Division.)	1	Southwest edge of Prémont (Aisne).	Small monument of cut stone.	1923	Erected by private subscription. Same design as 30th Div. monument. See picture on page 377.

526   MISCELLANEOUS

Unit or event commemorated	Number	Location	Character	Date erected	Remarks
118th Infantry. (30th Division.)	1	In the northern part of town of Brancourt-le-Grand (Aisne).	Small monument of cut stone.	1923	Erected by private subscription. Same design as 30th Div. monument. See picture on page 377.
310th Infantry. (78th Division.)	1	In church at town of Semur-en-Auxois (Côte-d'Or).	Stained-glass church window.	1927	In memory of the dead of the regiment.
313th Infantry. (79th Division.)	1	Alongside the road in old town of Montfaucon (Meuse).	Bronze tablet on a fence post.	Soon after the Armistice.	Tablet states that the town was captured by the regiment.
315th Infantry. (79th Division.)	1	Nantillois (Meuse).	Building given to the village as a recreation center.	1930	Erected by the regiment in memory of its dead. See picture appearing on page 525.
362d Infantry. (91st Division.)	1	Gesnes-en-Argonne (Meuse).	Concrete post, about 4 feet high.	Soon after the Armistice.	A small bronze plate describes fighting of regiment in vicinity.
371st Infantry. (93d Division.)	1	On hill in open field about ½ mile south of town of Ardeuil (Ardennes). (Difficult of access.)	Small granite monument, which lists names of the dead.	About 1924	In memory of the regiment's dead in vicinity. See the picture appearing on page 361.
372d Infantry. (93d Division.)	1	Along main road, ¼ mile south of Monthois (Ardennes).	Small obelisk of cut granite.	1920	In memory of members of the regiment killed in action, Sept. 26-Oct. 7, 1918. See picture on page 361.
6th Engineers.	1	Cathedral at Amiens (Somme).	Tablet.	1919	Erected by the citizens of Amiens to commemorate the dead of 6th Engineers lost in defense of that place.
23d Engineers.	1	In village of Varennes-en-Argonne (Meuse) across from the church.	Concrete marker, about 5 feet high.	Soon after the Armistice.	Erected by the men of the regiment.
The American Field Service.	1	At Pont-à-Mousson (Meurthe-et-Moselle).	Large Renaissance fountain.	1931	Erected by members of unit to those of American Field Service who died for France. See picture appearing on page 138.
The Lafayette Escadrille.	1	At Garches (Seine-et-Oise), near Paris.	Imposing memorial of cut stone.	1928	Erected by unit. Contains bodies of members. See the picture appearing on page 524.
All Pennsylvania troops who served in the World War.	1	At Varennes-en-Argonne (Meuse).	Development of a public park.	1927	Erected by the State of Pennsylvania. See picture on page 222.

MISCELLANEOUS   527

Unit or event commemorated	Number	Location	Character	Date erected	Remarks
Men of Missouri who gave their lives during the World War.	1	At the road junction, south of the town of Cheppy (Meuse).	Stone shaft surmounted by a bronze figure.	1922...........	Erected by the State of Missouri. See the picture on page 216.
To those of the U. S. Naval Air Station at Moutchic - Lacanau who lost their lives.	1	Moutchic (Gironde) west of Bordeaux.	Stone obelisk.......	Soon after the Armistice.	Erected by subscription from officers and men of naval air station. See the picture on page 524.
To those who were killed at Third Aviation Center.	1	11 kilometers from Issoudun (Indre), on road to Vatan, about 40 yards off from the road.	Stone, of medium size, surrounded by an iron chain on stone posts.	Soon after the Armistice.	Erected by subscription from officers who were on duty at the Aviation Center at the time. See the picture on page 524.
American soldiers who were killed at the village of Apremont.	1	Apremont (Meuse), near Montsec.	Building with a fountain outside.	1922...........	Erected with funds donated by the city of Holyoke, Massachusetts.
American soldiers who were killed near Seicheprey.	1	On outside of church in Seicheprey (Meurthe - et - Moselle), near door.	Small ornamental plaque of bronze.	1929...........	Funds were supplied by an American.
Achievements of American troops who fought in the vicinity of Sivry-sur-Meuse.	1	On the Borne de Cornouiller near Sivry-sur-Meuse. (Difficult of access.)	Stone obelisk.......	1925...........	See picture, page 524.
To the American volunteers who died for France.	1	In Place des Etats-Unis at Paris.	Stone, sculptured group on front.	1923...........	Erected by the French. American dead of the Foreign Legion. Lafayette Escadrille and American Field Service are listed. Picture on page 525.
To the first American troops to land in France.	1	St. Nazaire-sur-Loire (Loire Inférieure).	Stone shaft surmounted by a bronze soldier on an eagle's back.	1926...........	Erected by public subscription from Americans. See the picture appearing on page 524.
To first three Americans killed at front during the World War.	1	In Bathelémont (Meurthe-et-Moselle) 12 kilometers north of Lunéville.	Stone shaft, about 18 feet high.	1918...........	Erected by the French. See picture page 525.
Those who lost their lives as a result of the sinking of S. S. Tuscania during Feb. 5, 1918.	1	Near Islay, Scotland.	Stone tower on a rocky headland.	1920...........	Constructed by the American Red Cross not long after the war. See the picture appearing on page 524.

IV. American Memorials, Monuments and Cemeteries in Europe and the United States Not Associated with a Particular Battlefield

England

Surry

Brookwood American Cemetery

This 4.5-acre cemetery holds 468 graves and has the names of 563 of the missing-in-action (mostly naval) inscribed on the walls of its small classical-style chapel. The white marble Latin crosses (there is one Star of David headstone) are arranged in four sections around a central flagpole. One Medal of Honor recipient is buried here.

Brookwood cemetery is located in Surry just west of the town of Woking, west of London's ring road, the M25. It is most easily reached by automobile by leaving London on the M3, and then taking A322 south from Exit 3 for 5 miles. Trains for Brookwood leave from Waterloo Station in central London. The American cemetery is a 300-yard walk from the Brookwood train station.

Aldershot, home of the British Airborne Forces Museum, is 10 miles to the southwest.

Contact the staff at Brookwood American Cemetery, Dawney Hill-Brookwood, GU 240 JB. Woking, Surrey, UK. Phone: +44(0) 1483 473 237. GPS coordinates: N51 18.072 W0 38.430.

France

Paris

Le Château de Versailles: The Hall of Mirrors (Galerie des Glaces)

Of course Louis XIV's palace at Versailles is a world-class attraction in itself, aside from any connection it might have with the Great War. No visitor to Paris should miss the Château or its grounds. However, that said, the feature of the palace that is of greatest interest to WWI buffs is the Hall of Mirrors, a long, rectangular room (239.4′ x 34.4′) with 17 large, ornate arcaded mirrors facing opposing windows that look out on the gardens and has been used for ceremonial purposes since the reign of Louis XIV. Most of the actual negotiations over the articles of the famous treaty took place at the French Foreign Office, the Quai d'Orsay, but the formal signing took place on June 28, 1919 in the Hall of Mirrors to heighten the grandeur of the moment. None of the dignitaries present, Allied or German, could have missed the symbolism of Kaiser Wilhelm I, Chancellor Otto von Bismarck and Army Chief of Staff Helmuth von Moltke having triumphantly called the Second German Empire into being in this very hall after their 1871 victory in the Franco-Prussian War. Possibly that's a reason the Nazis didn't raise the Château in 1940 as they did the Clairière de l'Armistice.

When you plan your visit to the Château, we have a few suggestions that might make that experience more enjoyable.

Long gone are the summer days when you can simply walk up to the ticket window in the forecourt, buy your ticket and wander through the building. Single entry tickets can still be purchased that way, but you will invariably face a long ticket line, we mean really long. Instead of standing around all morning, we suggest that you book a tour (of which there are 74 choices currently available online) with a reputable agency that will take you out to Versailles from central Paris by bus or other private conveyance, allowing you to avoid parking problems and bypassing the long ticket lines. A tour ticket will also provide you with a knowledgeable guide who is guaranteed to make your visit more informative and enjoyable.

If you do decide to visit the Château on your own, the official website we list below will be invaluable in helping you plan your trip.

All of the Versailles attractions, which include Louis XIV's palace, the grounds surrounding it, the nearby Trianon palace and Marie-Antoinette's estate are open in the high season (April 1 to October 31) from 9 a.m. to 6:30 p.m. daily, except for Mondays and May 1. In the low season, the attractions close an hour earlier. Musical Fountain and Musical Garden shows are staged outside during the high season, weather permitting. Currently, the single ticket admission prices are 18 euros and 25 euros, the higher price including the Musical Fountain and Musical Garden shows. Of course, the price of a guided tour will be much higher. For additional, up-to-date-information go to the website: en.chateauversailles.fr .

Lafayette Escadrille Memorial
This memorial was dedicated in 1928 with private donations to honor the Lafayette Escadrille, the American volunteer aviation unit that joined the French before the U.S. entered the war. It consists of a white marble "Arc de Triomphe" flanked by loggias. The memorial contains 68 sarcophagi for the fliers who died, although only 49 actually hold remains. The empty tombs are for those killed whose bodies were never recovered.

The memorial was renovated in 2003 using a $2.1 million appropriation from the U.S. Congress.

The monument is located two stops further along the line from Suresnes at Garches-Marnes-la-Coquette. From the station it is approximately a quarter of a mile walk west to the Parc de Villeneuve-l'Etang, just beyond the Institut Pasteur.

By auto, exit the Paris périphérique by la Porte Saint- Cloud, and then pick up N307 (this section of the route carries various names honoring French military figures) to the Monument.

Suresnes American Cemetery and Memorial

This 7.5-acre cemetery is located in the suburb of Suresnes, 6.5 kilometers west of central Paris on the east slope of Mont Valérien. Opened in 1917 and dedicated on Memorial Day 1919 by President Woodrow Wilson, it holds the remains of 1,541 WWI dead and its walls bear the names of an additional 974 missing-in-action. Most of those interred here died of wounds or illness in military hospitals, many from the influenza epidemic of 1918-19. The chapel and additional landscaping were completed by the ABMC in 1934.

After WWII, the chapel was expanded by the addition of two loggias, one of which is dedicated to the memory of 24 unidentified dead from WWII. A white marble figure stands in each of the loggias to commemorate those buried and memorialized here. The loggia walls are inscribed with a summary of Americans lost in both World Wars and the location of American overseas military cemeteries. Charles A. Platt of New York designed the original chapel; his sons, William and Geoffrey, designed the post-WWII additions.

During WWII, the Nazi occupiers used the old Napoleonic-era fort on Mont Valérien as the execution site for some 4,500 French political prisoners and members of the Resistance. The French government has erected an impressive memorial to those victims on Mont Valérien that can also be visited along with the American cemetery.

You can access the Suresnes Cemetery from central Paris either by auto or by train. By auto, drive through the Bois de Boulogne on the Allée de Longchamp crossing the Seine over the Suresnes Bridge, and then bearing right following the signs to Mont Valérien. There is limited parking at the cemetery entrance.

Trains leave the Gare Saint-Lazare every 15 minutes for Suresnes. Leave the train station through the L'Hôpital Foch exit, turn right and walk to the Boulevard Washington. Turn right again and walk the 200 yards to the cemetery entrance (10-15 minutes).

Contact the staff at Suresnes American Cemetery, 123 Boulevard Washington, 92150 Suresnes, France. Phone: +33(0) 1 46 25 01 70. GPS coordinates: N48 52.314 E2 13.126.

Suresnes American Cemetery is just outside Paris.

Outside Paris

The American Monument at Meaux
This stunning 74.5 foot-high, seated figure of Marianne, symbol of the French nation, her head thrown back in anguish, holding a dead child in her lap, stands in an open park that allows the visitor an unfettered view.

The WWI Memorial in Atlantic City, N.J. has a 9-foot bronze replica.

For a more detailed description see our Eastern Tour, Day One.

Souilly Marker – 1st Army Headquarters

This weathered bronze tablet is attached to a wall of the Souilly Mairie (town hall). Souilly, a small town on the Voie Sacrée, now N35, is on the route that so many tens of thousands of French *poilus* traveled from the railhead at Bar-le-Duc to the killing fields at Verdun, never to return. Markers along the roadside trace this sacred way. The inscription on the plaque, in the shape of an urn, reads in English (with the French version alongside it):

> THE HEADQUARTERS
> OF THE AMERICAN FIRST ARMY
> OCCUPIED THIS BUILDING
> FROM SEPTEMBER 21, 1918
> TO THE END OF HOSTILITIES,
> AND FROM HERE CONDUCTED
> THE MEUSE-ARGONNE OFFENSIVE
> ONE OF THE GREAT OPERATIONS
> OF THE WORLD WAR
> ERECTED BY
> UNITED STATES OF AMERICA

The above inscription tells most of the story. Pétain had his HQ in this building during the siege of Verdun in 1916. Pershing and his staff made a point of visiting Verdun during their move from Chaumont to Souilly to pay their respects to the French sacrifice. Pershing kept his private train at a nearby siding during the Meuse-Argonne offensive, although it doesn't seem that he used it other than to entertain visitors.

To reach Souilly and travel a portion of the Voie Sacrée, exit the A4-E50 autoroute at Verdun (exit 30), and then drive a short distance south on N35. Verdun is 260 km from Paris by the A10 autoroute. GPS coordinates: N49 01.685 E17.159.

Tours American Monument

This Art Deco-style monument commemorates the work of the some 650,000 personnel of the AEF who worked in the Services of Supply (SOS), which was headquartered in Tours.

It consists of a lovely fountain surrounded by a small park just off the Avenue André Malraux, about 200 yards east of the southern end of the Pont Wilson, a bridge spanning the Loire River.

Surmounting the white stone fountain is a gilded statue of a crouching American-Indian with an eagle, wing upraised, perched on his arm. The square column on which he kneels has four bas-relief female figures on its sides representing the main divisions of the SOS: Administration, Construction, Procurement and Distribution. The coats-of-arms of French cities where the SOS maintained important installations are carved on the base beneath the catch basin.

The fountain is the work of architect Arthur Loomis Harmon, a member of the firm that designed the Empire State Building, and was dedicated on January 1, 1932.

Tours is 203 km from Paris by the A10 autoroute (Autoroute L'Aquitaine) on the way to Bordeaux and Spain. GPS coordinates: N47 23.842 E00 41. 337.

Spain

Naval Monument at Gibraltar

This memorial consists of an arch constructed of stone quarried from the "Rock" that leads to British North Front Cemetery, which is a site administered by the Commonwealth War Graves Commission. It is decorated with two large bronze seals, one of the United States and the other of the United States Navy. The inscription reads:

Erected by the United States of America
to commemorate the achievements and comradeship
of the British and American Navies in this vicinity during the
World War

Steps from the arch, located on the west side of Line Wall Road, lead down to the harbor. The bus stop on Routes 2, 3 and 4 is "American Steps."

United States

The United States World War One Centennial Commission maintains an extensive online list of known WWI memorials in the United States that now includes 100s of sites. Their listings are ongoing and especially useful because they include histories and descriptions of the memorials with map locations for reaching them. You can most easily search this database by clicking on the "Location Explorer" button and then, entering the name of the site (if you know it) or the name of the state in which it is located. See the Commission's website at www.worldwar1centennial.org.

The memorials listed below are only a sample of the many scattered throughout the country.

Atlantic City, N. J.

The state of New Jersey erected this memorial in 1922 to honor its citizens who died in the Great War. The memorial takes the form of a circular, colonnaded Greek temple standing in O'Donnell Memorial Park just off of Atlantic Avenue. A 9′ bronze reproduction of the Marianne statue located in Meaux, France, stands in the memorial's rotunda.

Denver, Colo.

There is a life-sized bronze statue of a doughboy in Denver's Fairmount Cemetery, one of the oldest in the city.

It stands guard over the grave of 2nd Lt. Francis Brown Lowry, who was a 23-year-old photographic observer in the 91st Observation Squadron, who died when his plane was downed by AA fire on September 26, 1918. Lowry's remains were reinterred in Denver in 1921, when the local Francis B. Lowry VFW post created the memorial. The recently-closed Lowry Air Force Base in Denver was named after him.

Dover, N. J.

This life-sized bronze statue of a doughboy, "The Spirit of the American Doughboy," stands in Hurd Park. It was sculpted by E.M. Viquesney and dedicated in 1922 to honor the 38 men from the Second District of Morris County who died in the Great War. Their names are on small plaques attached to stones around the statue's base.

Fort Riley, Kan.

There is a large stone obelisk Great War memorial on the Fort Riley grounds.

To visit the post, now home to the 1st ID, you will need to follow the DOD's regulations, which you can find at kansastravel.org/fortriley.htm or the Fort Riley website, riley.army.mil.

Doughboy stands guard over Lt. Francis Lowry's and other WW1 graves at Fairmount Cemetery in Denver, Colorado.

La Porte, Tex.

The dreadnought-era battleship, *USS Texas* (BB-35) is moored at La Porte just off the Houston ship channel adjacent to the San Jacinto battlefield and monument. The location is east of the city of Houston off I-10.

Texas was laid down in 1911 and commissioned in 1914. In 1918, she operated out of Scapa Flow with the Royal Navy's Grand Fleet. She was one of the battleships chosen to escort the German High Seas Fleet into its internment at Scapa Flow. *Texas* also fought in the 1942 North African campaign and in the 1944 trans-Pacific drive before she was decommissioned in 1948.

New York City, N.Y.

The 107th Infantry (the pre-war 7th New York National Guard Regiment) is commemorated by a monumental, larger-than-life, seven-figure bronze sculpture standing at the south end of Central Park near the intersection of Fifth Avenue and 67th Street. The work of sculptor Karl Illava, a sergeant in the 107th, the monument was dedicated in 1927. The 107th Infantry was paired with the 106th Infantry as the 54th Infantry Brigade of the 27th ID, one of only three divisions made up entirely of a single state's National Guard units. The 107th fought its major battles with the BEF in late 1918 at the St. Quentin Canal and beyond.

Dramatic monument dedicated to the 107th Infantry (Photo: Bruce Guthrie, www.bguthriephotos.com).

Washington, D.C., President's Park

1st Division Monument
This tall, slender white column surmounted by a figure representing victory stands in President's Park across from the Corcoran Gallery off 17th St., NW. It was dedicated in 1924 by the Society of the First Division and is today maintained by the National Park Service. In addition to the original dedication to those who fell in the Great War, plaques subsequently have been added to honor former members of the 1st ID who served in WWII, Vietnam and Desert Storm.

2nd Division Memorial
A dramatic memorial to all the men who have served in the "Indianhead Division" (so named because of the design of its insignia) also stands in President's Park. The memorial consists

of an upraised hand holding a gilded flaming sword framed by a flat arch. The memorial was designed by James E. Fraser and dedicated by President Roosevelt in 1936. As with the 1st Division memorial above, it has been updated to include soldiers who served in the division in subsequent wars.

————, Pershing Park

National WWI Memorial
Presently, plans are well underway to construct a WWI Memorial in Pershing Park, east of the White House off Pennsylvania Avenue. Completion of the Memorial is expected in 2018. See the Commission website for further details and for the opportunity to contribute to this memorial endeavor: www.worldwar1centennial.org. The park, which has existed since 1981, features a statue of Gen. Pershing by the sculptor Robert White, various memorial walls and a small pond that is converted to a skating rink in winter.

Washington State

Maryhill
This curious WWI memorial, in the form of a stylized version on England's Paleolithic Stonehenge, stands on the site of the town of Maryhill, Washington in the Columbia River valley. It was dedicated on November 11, 1929 to honor the military dead from Klickitat County.

This Stonehenge replica is located 105 miles east of Portland, Ore., off I-84.

V. Principal WWI Museums in the United States, Canada, Australia and Europe

Virtually all the nations that fought in the Great War later established museums, or added exhibits to existing museums, to commemorate their participation. The list below is hardly exhaustive, but it does highlight some of the best museums. We hope you will find it useful in investigating the multitude of artifacts that have survived the past century and that can make the horrific reality of life on the Western Front something more than a fading memory.

Most of the museums arranged below have adequate parking and food service, plus gift shops and bookstores. They are listed alphabetically by country and city.

Australia

Canberra

Australian War Memorial
The major WWI museum, opened in 1941, "holds one of the World's great collections of material related to the First World War," so says the blurb on its website. You only need a quick look at the exhibit descriptions to validate that claim. The entire west wing of the museum's ground floor is devoted to WWI exhibits of every category.

The Memorial is also the location of the country's Tomb of the Unknown Australian Soldier that was dedicated on November 11, 1993. It holds the remains of an unknown Australian "Digger" reinterred from the Adelaide Cemetery in France.

At the end of each day, 4:55 p.m. to be exact, the Memorial stages an impressive "Last Post" ceremony, which echoes the poignant British ceremony held a world away each evening at the Menin Gate near Ypres, Belgium.

The Memorial is located off the Treloar Crescent in Canberra. Open: 10:00 a.m. to 5:00 p.m. daily. Closed on Christmas Day. Much more information is found on the Memorial's website: www.awm.gov.au.

Austria

Vienna

The Museum of Military History (Heeresgeschichtliches Museum)

This outstanding museum covers all phases of the military history of the Austrian Empire and its successors since the Thirty Years War. It is housed in the 19th century Arsenal in the heart of Vienna.

Along with numerous other phases of Austrian military history, there are halls devoted to:

WWI and the End of the Habsburg Monarchy
The Austrian Navy
Artillery
Military Aviation
and – a Tank Garden outside

The museum is open daily 9:00 a.m. to 5:00 p.m. except for New Year's Day, Easter Sunday, May 1, Nov. 1, Dec. 25 and 31. Regular admission starts at 6 euros; admission is free on the 1st Sundays of every month and on Dec. 26. The museum can be contacted at www.hgm.at.

Belgium

Brussels

Royal Museum of the Armed Forces and Military History

According to its website, the museum's number 14-18 Galleries exhibit the "biggest and most diverse collection … in the world" of WWI artifacts.   Of the Great War belligerents, only Greece and Bulgaria are not represented. The displays include military aircraft, weapons and vehicles with the signage mostly in French.

The museum, located in the Parc du Cinquantenaire in the heart of Brussels, is open daily 9:00 a.m. to 5:00 p.m., except Mondays. Admission charged; bank and credit cards are accepted.

The museum maintains a WWI site just outside Brussels named the "Trench of Death," which gives the visitor a chance to visit a beautifully restored trench line without the inconvenience of machine gun and artillery fire, to say nothing of gas attacks.

Canada

Ottawa

The Canadian War Museum

During its World War I Centenary, the Canadian War Museum will showcase a number of exhibits in 2017 including one on the Battle of Vimy Ridge and another on "War and the Media." The series will continue through 2019.

The museum is centrally located on the banks of the Ottawa River. Its opening and closing times are complicated, but it is generally open daily in the summer from 9:30 a.m. to 6:00 p.m. with the closing time shortened by an hour in winter. It is closed on Christmas Day and from January 9-13 for annual maintenance. Check its website at warmuseum.ca for more details. Admission charged. Phone: 1-800-555-5621.

France

Meaux

Musée de la Grande Guerre du Pays de Meaux

This WWI museum opened a few years ago in a modern building located in the northern part of the city next to "The American Monument," thus making it possible to visit both on the same excursion from Paris. The exhibits, based on a private collection, are extensive and professionally displayed. It is well worth a visit.

Details about the unusual "American Monument" are covered in our sections dealing with non-battle or battlefield memorials and the Eastern tour.

Meaux is easily accessible from Paris by train; then, a cab is your simplest option to reach the museum. The trip from Paris Est takes about half-an-hour and the trains run all day.

If you decide to drive, take N3 out of Paris to the major roundabout on the outskirts of Meaux, which you leave on D1005 to the north. Follow your Google Earth or GPS directions to the park.

Paris

Musée de l'Armée

This world-class museum is located in the Hôtel des Invalides in central Paris. Three rooms in the Contemporary Department, The Two World Wars, 1871-1945, are devoted to WWI: the Joffre Room, the Poilus Room and the Foch Room. While you are in the Invalides do not miss Napoleon's tomb and that of Marshal Foch in the Church of the Dome.

The museum is open daily from 10:00 a.m. to 6:00 p.m. in the summer; it closes at 5:00 p.m. in the winter. There is actually a rather complicated schedule of days when the museum (or parts of the museum) is closed. Consult its website for details: musee-armee.fr. Admission charged.

Musée de l'Air et de l'Espace, Le Bourget

This north Paris museum is located on the old Le Bourget airfield that became world-famous in 1927 when Charles Lindbergh landed there after his solo transatlantic flight.

Today, the field is the site of a major air and space museum that houses a collection of WWI aircraft in its Hall 2, "Les as de 14-18."

The museum is open six days a week (closed Mondays) from 10:00 a.m. to 6:00 p.m. in summer and closes an hour earlier in winter. It is also closed Christmas and New Year's Days. Admission charged.

Le Bourget can be reached by auto in about 10 minutes from the A1 autoroute and by various means of public transportation. See its website for details: museeairespace.fr.

Verdun

Le Mémorial de Verdun

This major WWI museum reopened in 2016 after a thorough renovation. Its collection contains artifacts, weapons, uniforms and documents relating to the 1916 battle. Verdun is an essential stop on any tour of WWI sites and Mémorial should not be missed if you are in the city. Le Mémorial also offers guided tours of the battlefield.

Le Mémorial is open daily from 9:30 a.m. to 5:00 p.m. in winter and from 9:30 to 7:00 in summer. Annual closure runs from December 23 through to the end of January. Admission charged.

For more information go to its website: memorial-verdun.fr. Phone: +33 (0)3 29 84 35 34.

Great Britain

Biggleswade, Bedfordshire

Old Warden Aerodrome, The Shuttleworth Collection
Richard O. Shuttleworth, aviation and racing enthusiast, began his eclectic collection of vintage aircraft, motorcycles, bicycles and vintage automobiles in the early 20th century. The collection now includes 58 aircraft dating from the mid-1890s (gliders) to WWII. Included are a number of WWI era aircraft, including a Sopwith Pup, Triplane and Camel. Some of the aircraft are originals; others are flying replicas.

Old Warden Aerodrome is about 50 miles north of London off the A1 motorway.

For further information about the collection go to enquire@shuttleworth.org. Phone: +44 (0) 1767 627 927. Admission charged.

Edinburgh

The Scottish National War Museum
The National War Museum encompasses the entire gamut of Scottish war-making, which has been considerable. It mounts temporary WWI exhibits along with permanent ones. The

museum is located at the top of the Royal Mile, inside Edinburgh Castle in central Edinburgh. It is open daily from 9:45 a.m. to 5:45 p.m. from April through September with the time shortened by an hour during the rest of the year. The museum is closed on December 25-26. Admission to the War Museum is included in the admission charge for the Castle. For additional information go to: www.nms.ac.uk/national-war-museum.

Greenwich

The National Maritime Museum

The National Maritime Museum, the world's premier maritime and naval museum, has several exhibits featuring the naval history of WWI, a current one titled "Jutland 1916: WWI's Greatest Sea Battle."

The museum is open daily from 10:00 a.m. to 6:00 p.m. in summer with the time shortened by an hour in winter. It is closed on December 24-26. Admission free. For additional information go to: www.vmg.co.uk.

London

In London, the two "not to miss" museums are the Imperial War Museum and the RAF Museums at Hendon (north London).

The Imperial War Museum

The IWM London features many galleries housing permanent WWI displays, while its Duxford Annex near Cambridge has an extensive collection of aircraft, but does not specialize in WWI types.

IWM London is open from 10:00 a.m. to 6:00 p.m. daily, except for December 24, 25 and 26. Admission free. The museum can be reached easily by 10-minute walks from the

Elephant & Castle, Waterloo or Lambeth North Underground Stations. Website: iwm.org.uk. Phone: +44 (0) 20 7416 5000.

The Royal Air Force Museums, Hendon and Cosford Annex

The RAF Museum at the old Hendon Aerodrome in north London is the home of an impressive collection of 14 WWI aircraft making it a must stop for the WWI aviation buff.

Three other WWI aircraft (a Sopwith Pup and 11/2 Strutter and a Bristol M1c) are displayed at the Museum's Cosford Annex near Shifnal, Shropshire (about 27 miles northwest of Birmingham).

Currently, the Hendon museum has mounted an exhibit entitled "The First World War in the Air," along with a series of more temporary exhibits.

You can visit the RAF Museums in Hendon by taking the Edgeware branch of the Northern Line to the Colindale Underground Station, and then walking or taking a cab or bus to the complex. It is a substantial hike, so consider that cab if your time and energy are limited.

The Grahame-White Factory building, where the WWI exhibits are located, is open in the summer from 10:00 a.m. to 6:00 p.m. and 10:00 a.m. to 5:00 p.m. in the winter. Admission free. Website: rafmuseum.org.uk. Phone: +44 (0) 020 8205 2266 (Hendon); +44 (0) 190 2376 200 (Cosford).

Italy

Rovereto

Museo Storico Italiano della Guerra

This outstanding museum tucked away in Rovereto, 27 km south of Trento in northern Italy, has extensive exhibits of period small arms, artillery, military vehicles, uniforms and even projectiles used by the Italian army in the Great War. The museum also exhibits artifacts dealing with Italy's colonial wars and its participation in WWII. It's a "must stop" on a northern trip to Trento or nearby Lake Garda.

The museum is located in the ancient Castle, just off SS46, on the via Vicenza, on the east side of Rovereto. It is open every day except Monday (open then on bank holidays) from 10:00 a.m. to 6 p.m. (7 p.m. in summer). For more information visit its website: info@museodellaguerra.it; Phone: +39 0464 438700.

United States

Chicago, Ill.

Pritzker Military Museum & Library

This privately maintained library and museum opened in 2003 with the goals of acquiring, maintaining and making accessible a large variety of materials focusing on the history of the citizen soldier in the United States. The collection is based on items originally donated by its founder, Col. J. N. Pritzker.

In addition to its library and artifact collection, the museum supports a wide variety of programs and events that include collecting oral interviews with Medal of Honor recipients and hosting over 400 events since its opening involving lectures and discussions with scholars, active military personnel and authors. The Pritzker also sponsors a book club and rents space for private events.

The museum is located at 104 S. Michigan Ave., Chicago, Ill. 60603 and opens daily at 10:00 a.m. (12:00 p.m. on Sunday), closing at 4 p.m. or 6 p.m. depending on the day. Admission charged to non-members. Website: pritzkermilitary.org. Phone: (312) 374 9333.

Dayton, Ohio.

National Museum of the USAF, Wright-Patterson AFB

The Air Force Museum sponsors a WWI Dawn Patrol every other year that features flying WWI military aircraft reproductions and WWI re-enactors. In 2016, the event was held during the first two days of October. The museum is also planning a centennial exhibition about aviation in the Great War.

The museum is open daily from 9:00 a.m. to 5:00 p.m. Closed on Thanksgiving, Christmas and New Year's Days. Admission free. Website: www.nationalmuseum.af.mil

Kansas City, Mo.

National WWI Museum of the United States (formerly the Liberty Memorial)

Fundraising for the "Liberty Memorial" began a year after the guns fell silent on the Western Front. Groundbreaking occurred on November 1, 1921, and the neo- Egyptian-style building with its 265-foot tower, was dedicated on November 11, 1926.

In 2004, the Memorial was re-designated as the "National WWI Museum of the United States" and two years later it was given the status of National Historic Landmark. More recently, President Barack Obama signed a bill designating the museum a "National Memorial."

The Museum's Main Gallery has a permanent exhibit entitled "The World War, 1914-1919." Temporary exhibits drawn from the museum's collection of 100,000 objects and documents are located in side galleries. The museum also has a dining facility known as the Over There Café.

The museum's regular hours, Tuesday through Sunday, are 10:00 a.m. to 5:00 p.m.; it opens an hour earlier on Saturday. It is closed on Mondays except for holiday Mondays and during the summer; also closed on Thanksgiving, Christmas Eve and Day, New Year's Day and May 14. Admission charged. Website: theworldwar.org. Phone: 816-888-8100.

Rhinebeck, N.Y.

Old Rhinebeck Aerodrome

The airfield at Rhinebeck, N.Y. features flyable WWI aircraft reproductions in its weekend air shows. The aircraft include both a Fokker Dr.1 and a D.VII. It is possible to actually go up in one of these planes.

Rhinebeck is located about ten miles north of Poughkeepsie off the Albany Post Road (Highway 9) on the east side of the Hudson River. Check the Rhinebeck Aerodrome website, oldrhinebeck.org, for details.

Washington, D.C.

The Library of Congress

The Library of Congress is currently mounting two temporary exhibits on the Great War: the multi-format "Echoes of the Great War" (to 1/31/19) and "World War I: American Artists View the Great War" (to 8/19/17). Both are located in the Graphic Arts Galleries, Ground Floor, Thomas Jefferson Building. Open from 8:30 a.m. to 5:00 p.m. Monday through Saturday. Closed on Thanksgiving, Christmas and New Year's Day. For further information go to loc.gov.

The Smithsonian Institution

American History Museum, The National Mall

The American History Museum has a permanent exhibit entitled "The Price of Freedom: Americans at War," which has the

206 | The Great Crusade

carrier pigeon Cher Ami, made famous by the ordeal of "The Lost Battalion," on display. This exhibit is located on the 3rd Floor of the East Wing.

The museum is mounting an exhibition in the spring of 2017: "Modern Medicine and the Great War."

The AHM is open from 10:00 a.m. to 5:30 p.m. daily, except for Christmas Day. Admission free.

National Air and Space Museum, The National Mall

The Smithsonian's main collection of WWI military aircraft is located at the Air and Space museum on the Mall. It consists of a number of original Allied and German aircraft with associated displays, making it one of the most important in the world. The exhibit, "Legends, Memory, and the Great War in the Air," is located on the 2nd floor of the West Wing. Among the aircraft displayed are a Spad XIII, a Sopwith 7F.1 Snipe and a Fokker D.VII. A small theater also runs a video presentation about the air war.

The museum is mounting an exhibit of WWI posters in the spring of 2017.

The Steven F. Udvar-Hazy Center, Chantilly, Va.

The Smithsonian's Air and Space Museum Annex, the Udvar-Hazy Center, located in Chantilly, Va. near Dulles International Airport, exhibits a small collection of WWI aircraft, including a Spad XVI and a Nieuport 28 C.1 (tricked out in 94th Aero Squadron colors), both types flown by American pilots. One of Capt. Eddie Rickenbacker's (the top American ace) uniforms is also on display.

The museums are open every day, except for Christmas from 10:00 a.m. to 5:30 p.m. Admission is free. See the Smithsonian's excellent website, airandspace.si.edu, for further information.

U. S. Navy Museum, Washington Navy Yard
This museum has a permanent display on the U. S. Navy in WWI that includes one of the rail cars that once mounted a 14″ gun used in the Meuse-Argonne Offensive. Unfortunately, it's now difficult for the casual tourist to gain admittance to the Washington Navy Yard. Visitors must have DOD credentials or be with someone who does. If you are 18 or over, you must present a photo ID as well. Check history.navy.mil for details.

West Point, N.Y.

West Point Museum
The West Point Museum, located on the grounds of the U. S. Military Academy, has mounted an exhibit entitled "American Propaganda during World War I: Championing a Nation" that examines the role of George Creel's Committee on Public Information in influencing public opinion. The powerful German telescope that sat on top of Montfaucon was once in the museum's collection, but unfortunately disappeared during WWII.

The museum is open daily from 10:30 a.m. to 4:15 p.m. Closed Thanksgiving, Christmas and New Year's Days. Check to see if there are any special regulations governing admission to the post. Admission free. Website: www.westpoint.army.mil.htl

Wheaton, Ill.

1st Division Museum at Cantigny Park
Wheaton is home to the country estate of Col. Robert R. McCormick, former publisher of the "Chicago Tribune," who named his estate "Cantigny" because he fought there with the 1st ID as an artillery officer.

The 1st Division Museum, located in Cantigny Park, has 10,000 sq. ft. of display space as well as a tank park with one example of a WWI tank. (The French WWI tank on display inside is a wooden replica.)

The museum will be closed after November 11, 2016 for renovation, but is scheduled to reopen in the summer of 2017. It has been traditionally open from May 1 to October 1, Tuesday-Sunday, 10 a.m. to 5 p.m.; the remainder of the year it closes an hour earlier. Website: www.fdmuseum.org

VI. WWI at the Movies

A quick Google search will show you that there is no dearth of WWI films or lists of choices for the best ones. Google www.ranker.com, www.indiewire.com or www.wikipedia.org for examples. As you might expect, the majority of the films, especially the great ones, don't deal with the AEF; the American involvement in the war was just too brief. Still, Hollywood was off the mark quickly rushing a silent film on the Lost Battalion (the first of three) into the theaters in 1919. There has been a steady trickle of films coming out of studios around the world ever since. The next few years will probably see more than a few hit the silver screen.

First, we want to highlight three of our favorites, films that don't even remotely deal with the AEF, before listing many other excellent ones, some of which do.

Right at the top of our list are three great films: "All Quiet on the Western Front" (1930); "Paths of Glory" (1957); and "Lawrence of Arabia" (1962).

Lewis Milestone's anti-war adaptation of Erich Maria Remarque's novel "All Quiet of the Western Front" is the earliest. The 1930 film, starring Lew Ayres as the anti-war, long-suffering *Soldat* Paul Baumer, was a sobering antidote for American wartime, anti-German hysteria.

The current DVD features the film in a version carefully restored by The Library of Congress film department. Nevertheless, it's still an 87-year-old production that suffers from cinema's recent emergence from the silent era. It set the basic format for countless WWII films to come.

Stanley Kubrick's 1958 black and white (in the Technicolor era) takes on the insanity of war and specifically this war, "Paths of Glory," looks at the absurdity of trench warfare from a cynical French perspective. Kirk Douglas as Col. Dax, Adolphe Menjou as Gen. Broulard and Ralph Meeker as Corp. Paris turn in memorable performances. The film ends with a moving scene in which the stunning actress, Christiane Harlan, the only female in the cast, sings "The Faithful Hussar" to sooth a roomful of drunken *poilus*. Note: the film was banned in France for 20 years during which Harlan and Kubrick enjoyed their lifelong marriage.

David Lean's great epic, "Lawrence of Arabia," is often overlooked as a WWI film, yet it is possibly the best, and made T. E. Lawrence, along with actors Peter O'Toole and Omar Sharif, famous to worldwide audiences. The film was nominated for ten Oscars, winning seven, but not the Best Actor or Supporting Actor awards for O'Toole and Sharif. Whether the film is an accurate portrayal of Lawrence is almost beside the point. His brother said that O'Toole had turned in a magnificent performance as "Ned", but it was not a true portrait of his brother. In any case, it was a box office hit that defines what most of the world knows about the Arab Revolt during The Great War. Its popularity continues unabated; there have been five DVD editions. The latest enhanced Blu-ray-version, containing new footage that originally landed on the cutting room floor, was released in 2012 on its 50th anniversary, receiving a brief theatrical release in the U.S. and Canada.

After these top three, you can dip into the extensive film library to suit your taste. If you like aviation films, give "Wings" (1927, silent), "Hell's Angels" (1930) or "The Blue Max" (1966) a look. The latter film stars a top tier (for 1966) cast featuring George Peppard, James Mason and Ursula Andress. Erich von Stroheim fans will want to view "La Grande Illusion" (1937). If you favor the American experience, try sharing a French cellar with marines Jimmy Cagney and Dan Dailey in "What Price Glory" (1954), a remake of the 1926 silent film based on Laurence Stallings and Maxwell Anderson's 1924 stage play, or open warfare in the Argonne Forest with Gary Cooper in

"Sergeant York" (1940) or life with three doughboys in Laurence Stallings' "The Big Parade" (1925). Cooper appears with Helen Hayes in a less stoic role in an adaptation of Ernest Hemingway's anti-war novel, "A Farewell to Arms" (1932). "The Fighting 69th" (1940) depicts the New York 69th Infantry Regiment in action. It starred James Cagney, Pat O'Brien and George Brent as "Wild Bill" Donovan. The latest acclaimed version of "Galloping Charlie" Whittlesey's stand with the Lost Battalion is a 2002 A&E made-for-TV effort titled (of course) "The Lost Battalion." Mel Gibson poignantly captures the Australian experience in "Gallipoli" (1981). Katharine Hepburn finds love with Humphrey Bogart in "The African Queen" (1951), a brilliant film that concerns itself with perseverance and love in wartime Africa.

More recently, "Flyboys," (2006) starring James Franco, depicted Americans who volunteered to become fighter pilots in the Lafayette Escadrille. The film, which was a box-office flop, ends with an epilogue that tells of the fate of each pilot depicted in the movie.

Another newer film, Steven Spielberg's "War Horse" (2011) has brought us face-to-face with the horror of using horses and other beasts-of-burden in a war dominated by barbed wire, machine guns and artillery, a practice that was still common twenty years later in WWII.

Screenwriter Dalton Trumbo's "Johnny Got His Gun" (1971), his open return to the film world after being blacklisted by Hollywood, confronts the hospital existence of a wounded doughboy and is not for the squeamish.

If you are fond of comedies, you are seriously out of luck, but you might try "The Life and Death of Colonel Blimp" (1943), sometimes titled simply "Colonel Blimp." It stars a very young Deborah Kerr (22) and touches on Blimp's tragicomic career in WWI.

In 1969, Richard Attenborough directed a British, anti-war film, "Oh! What a Lovely War", based on a 1963 stage musical by the same name, that assembled a remarkable cast of actors in guest roles: Sir Laurence Olivier, Vanessa and Michael Redgrave, John Mills, Susannah York and Maggie Smith to name the best-known. The songs used in both productions are those popular during the war.

This list could go on for pages, but the above films are among the best war films ever made and, in some cases, the very best films ever made. Almost all are anti-war and shocking in their depiction of WWI combat. Most are available through film rental services such as Netflix.

BIBLIOGRAPHY:
A SHORT READING LIST

We have put together a short list of books about WWI from the thousands that have been published. Many more will appear in the next two years as we pass through the 100th anniversary of the War. We have limited our bibliography mostly to recent and printed secondary popular histories that we feel will interest the general reader, so you will not find citation to the U.S. Army multi-volume histories of the war. Many of these secondary works have extensive bibliographies that will allow you to pursue the AEF's history in much more detail.

GENERAL HISTORIES
Still extremely readable is James Stokesbury's *A Short History of World War I* (1981). More recently a number of large-format books have appeared replete with exquisitely drawn maps and an abundance of photographs. Among the most useful are John Keegan's *An Illustrated History of the First World War* (2001) and H. P. Willmott, *World War I* (2003). An interesting way to view the war is through Martin Gilbert's *Atlas of the First World War: The Complete History* (1970, 1994) that features 164 maps illustrating all phases. Gilbert also published a standard history of the war titled *The First World War: A Complete History* (1994). Scott Addington has produced a unique little volume for casual reader in an effort to make "a very daunting subject easier to digest and understand" entitled *The First World War: A*

Layman's Guide (2014). If what you want are the essentials, presented in a colloquial style without the distraction of maps or page and chapter numbers, then this is your book.

None of these works expend many words on the AEF or the American war effort.

THE COMING OF WAR

Barbara W. Tuchman's *The Guns of August* (1962) is the classic and very readable account of the opening phases of the Great War. She followed the success of her first book with *The Proud Tower: A Portrait of the World Before the War, 1890-1914* (1966*)*, an examination of the European social and political order on the eve of war and *The Zimmermann Telegram* (1966).

Robert Ferrell has a chapter on America's entry into the war in his *American Diplomacy* (1975). The older, standard diplomatic histories of the United States by Thomas A. Bailey and Samuel F. Bemis do the same.

Capt. "Blinker" Hall's involvement in the Zimmermann telegram affair is treated at length in Patrick Beesly's *Room 40* (1982). *Dead Wake: The Last Crossing of the Lusitania* (2015) by Erik Larson is a detailed and fascinating account of that fateful Atlantic passage. An earlier, more thorough treatment with many fascinating photographs is Diana Preston's *Lusitania: An Epic Tragedy* (2002).

One look at George Creel's Committee on Public Information's ongoing propaganda efforts to sell the war to the American people is Alfred E. Cornebise's *War As Advertised: The Four Minute Men and America's Crusade 1917-1918* (1984). It examines the way in which Americans were "cajoled, coaxed, exhorted, wheedled, stimulated and inspired" into supporting the war effort by these patriotic speakers, which included dampening resistance to the draft among the nation's 17 million foreign born. Cornebise has also contributed a volume discussing the unique efforts the AEF made to further the education of American soldiers stuck in France in 1919 awaiting transport back to the United States in *Soldier-Scholars: Higher Education in the AEF, 1917-1919* (1997).

THE CREATION OF THE AEF

The creation and deployment of the AEF is examined at length in Russell E. Weigley's *History of the United States Army* 1984). Edward M. Coffman's *The War to End All Wars: The American Military Experience in World War I* (1986) is the standard monograph that covers the creation of the AEF and its battles in some detail.

GUIDES

Two works by individuals who have recently visited WWI battlefield sites are Gene Smith's *Still Quiet on the Western Front* (1965) and Stephen O'Shea's *Back to the Front* (1996). Neither book, great reads that they are, is very useful to travelers primarily interested in AEF sites, nor is Rose E. B. Coombs' *Before Endeavours Fade* (1983). More recent guides by Major Tonie Holt and his wife, Valmai Holt, are of course more comprehensive, but not much better; they are easily available from Amazon: Maj. and Mrs. Holt's *The Western Front – South: Battlefield Guide* (2006) and also *The Western Front – North: Battlefield Guide* (2014).

The official American battlefield guide is: *American Armies and Battlefields in Europe* (1995), now published by the U.S. Army's Center of Military History. It's a reprint of the 1938 guide, which itself was based on an earlier 1927 version (*A Guide to the American Battle Fields in Europe*) that Maj. Dwight D. Eisenhower researched and wrote for Gen. Pershing's American Battle Monuments Commission. Today's reprint is obviously dated and its maps are virtually unusable without 20/20 vision and a high degree of map reading skill, still it's a valuable resource.

David C. Homsher's *American Battlefields of World War I: Château-Thierry — Then and Now, Vol. I: Enter the Yanks* (2006) takes a rambling look at the actions of the 2nd and 3rd IDs around the town with special emphasis on medical units and field hospitals, often neglected topics.

BATTLES

Volume II of Frederic L. Paxson's *America at War: 1917-1918* (3 vols; 1939) has long been the standard work on the AEF.

Laurence Stallings, a marine junior officer wounded during the fighting in the Belleau Wood (he later lost a leg as a result), published a valuable account of the AEF entitled *The Doughboys: The Story of the AEF, 1917-1918* (1963).

Edward Coffman's history cited earlier covers the AEF's major battles. *Yanks: The Epic Story of the American Army in World War I* (2001) by John S. D. Eisenhower is a concise, very readable account with outstanding maps. The more recent *The American Army and the First World War* (2014) by David R. Woodward, a volume in a series on WWI armies, takes a hard look at the AEF, both its successes and failures.

Mark Grotelueschen's *AEF Way of War: The American Army and Combat in World War I* (2007) is invaluable in understanding the transition from "open warfare" doctrine to the more realistic "trench warfare" practice in the AEF during the summer and fall of 1918. The 1st ID at Cantigny is the subject of a detailed chapter by Allan R. Millett in Charles E. Heller and William A. Stofft's *America's First Battles* (1986). Recently, Matthew J. Davenport has reexamined the battle in *First Over There: The Attack on Cantigny, America's First Battle of World War I* (2015).

Nimrod T. Frazer's *Send the Alabamians: WWI Fighters in the Rainbow Division* (2014) retells the battles of the 167th Infantry (42nd ID), including that at the Croix Rouge Farm.

For St. Mihiel and the Metz option see James H. Hallas, *Squandered Victory: The American First Army at St. Mihiel* (1995).

Soissons, 1918 (1999) by Douglas, V. Johnson, II and Rolfe L. Hillman, Jr. is the one available study of the battle.

Inevitably, The AEF greatest battle between the Argonne Forest and the Meuse has attracted the most attention from historians. Historian Robert H. Ferrell has contributed two studies — *America's Deadliest Battle: Meuse-Argonne, 1918* (2007) and *Five Days in October: The Lost Battalion of World War I* (2005). The excellent *To Conquer Hell: The Meuse-Argonne, 1918, The Epic Battle That Ended The First World War* (2009) by Edward G. Lengel is another recent study. Mitchell Yockelson's *Forty-Seven Days: How Pershing's Warriors Came of Age to Defeat the German Army in World War I* (2016) adds to the growing stack.

Besides Ferrell's account cited above, Whittlesey's stand is the subject of Thomas M. Johnson and Fletcher Pratt's *The Lost Battalion* (1938, 2000 reprint). The life and combat exploits of the legendary Sgt. York gets a new treatment in Douglas V. Mastriano's *Alvin York: A New Biography of the Hero of the Argonne* (2014). Mastriano make a convincing case that he located the exact spot in the Argonne Forest where York performed his incredible feats of marksmanship.

William Walker takes a revisionist look at the 79th ID's actions in the offensive that is highly critical of Robert Lee Bullard's generalship in his *Betrayal at Little Gibraltar: A German Fortress, a Treacherous American General and the Battle to End World War I* (2016).

THE ARMISTICE

The Armistice is the subject of Stanley Weintraub's *A Stillness Heard Around the World: The End of the Great War: November*

1918 (1985). Joseph Persico uses the events leading up to November 11 as a way of addressing the history of the war from its beginning in his *Eleventh Month, Eleventh Day, Eleventh Hour: Armistice Day 1918: World War I and Its Violent Climax.* (2004).

UNIT HISTORIES

Many of the American divisions that fought on the Western Front published accounts of their actions shortly after the war. We have counted a total of 21, but that number shouldn't be considered complete. The division histories we found are for the following units: Regular Army – 1st, 2nd, 3rd, 4th and 5th; National Guard – 26th (3), 27th, 32nd, 33nd, 35th, 36th, 37th and 42nd; Draftee Army – 77th, 79th, 82nd, 89th, 90th and 91st. In addition, there are a number of regimental histories, but none we have found for the Armies or Corps, given their temporary existence.

MEMOIRS

Many senior officers wrote their memoirs, among them John J. Pershing, James G. Harbord, Robert L. Bullard, Hunter Liggett, Douglas MacArthur and George C. Marshall. Lt. Laurence Stallings published an autobiographical novel after the war entitled *Plumes* (1925). Francis P. Duffy, much beloved Catholic chaplain for the 26th Infantry, contributed his fresh memories of the fighting in *Father Duffy's Story* (1919). Among Frederick Palmer's various works on the war, his personal account, *With My Own Eyes: A Personal Story of the Battle Years* (1933), is very readable. Palmer was a war correspondent and member of Pershing's staff who also wrote biographies of the "Big Chief," Newton Baker and Tasker Bliss. Former marine Lieutenant John W. Thomason gave us his eyewitness account of Senegalese tactics in *Fix Bayonets!* (1926). A. Scott Berg's *World War I and America: Told By the Americans Who Lived It*

(2017) is an anthology of letters and writing coming out of the war years.

BIOGRAPHIES

Naturally more biographies have been written about Pershing than any other AEF figure. They began appearing just after the war ended and there have been a trickle ever since. The current standard work is Frank E. Vandiver's two-volume *Black Jack: The Life and Times of John J. Pershing* (1977). More recently several shorter studies of the AEF commander have appeared including Gene Smith, *Until the Last Trumpet Sounds* (1998), which moves through the war years quickly, Jim Lacey's *Pershing: A Biography* (2008) and John Perry's *Pershing: Commander of the Great War* (2011), the last two of which are quick reads because of their brevity. Allan R. Millet treats the career of Gen. Robert L. Bullard in *The General: Robert L. Bullard and Officership in the United States Army 1881-1925* (1975).

Other AEF figures who have received biographical treatments are George C. Marshall, George S. Patton, Douglas MacArthur, Tasker H. Bliss, Peyton C. Marsh, Newton D. Baker, William L. "Billy" Mitchell, Alvin York, Sam Woodfill and Harry S. Truman to list a number of familiar personages.

LAST WORDS

We can't end this reading list without mentioning one of the great works on the war, Paul Fussell's *The Great War and Modern Memory* (1975), an effort to interpret the shattering impact of the war through the literature it inspired from four British writers and poets: Robert Graves, Wilfred Owen, Edmund Blunden and Siegfried Sassoon (with side glances at a few lesser writers). It is a tour-de-force in literary criticism and provides a unique insight into the universal impact of the war on those who experienced it.

ABOUT THE AUTHORS

Stephen T. Powers

Professor Stephen T. Powers is the author of The March to Victory: A Guide to World War II Battles and Battlefields from London to the Rhine. Along with Kevin Dennehy, he is the author of The D-Day Assault: A 70th Anniversary Guide to the Normandy Landings and Finding Custer – An American Icon's Journey from West Point to the Little Bighorn. A U.S. Naval Academy graduate, Powers was a history professor at the University of Northern Colorado for more than 30 years.

Kevin Dennehy

Kevin Dennehy has been a journalist for more than 30 years, writing for daily newspapers, magazines and online publications. A retired Army National Guard colonel, Dennehy is a veteran of combat tours in Afghanistan and Iraq.

For book updates and our blog, go to:
www.militaryhistorytraveler.com.

NOTES